INVISIBLE LIGHT

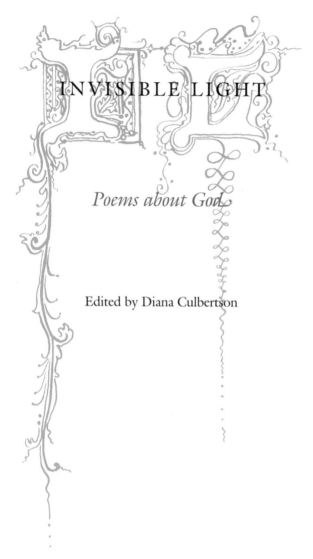

INVISIBLE LIGHT

Poems about God

Edited by Diana Culbertson

COLUMBIA UNIVERSITY PRESS

NEW YORK

COLUMBIA UNIVERSITY PRESS

Publishers Since 1893

New York   Chichester, West Sussex

Copyright © 2000 Columbia University Press

All rights reserved

Library of Congress Cataloging-in-Publication Data

Invisible Light : poems about God / edited by Diana Culbertson.

p.   cm.

ISBN 0-231-12062-1

1. God—Poetry. 2. Religious poetry, English. 3. Religious poetry, American.

I. Culbertson, Diana.

PR1191 .I6 2000

821.008'0382—dc21

00-035850

Casebound editions of Columbia University Press books are
printed on permanent and durable acid-free paper.

Printed in the United States of America

Designed by Linda Secondari

Illustrations by Martha Lewis

c 10 9 8 7 6 5 4 3 2 1

And when we have built an altar to the Invisible Light,
 we may set thereon the little lights for which our
 bodily vision is made.
And we thank Thee that darkness reminds us of light.
O Light Invisible, we give Thee thanks for Thy great glory!
            —T. S. ELIOT, Choruses from *The Rock* (10)

"Our gaze is submarine," wrote T. S. Eliot in a chorus from "The Rock," a poem that praises all light and acknowledges that darkness reminds us of light. St. Paul understood the same truth: "For now we see in a mirror dimly. . . ." The awareness that God is not perceived "face to face" but only through reflections is fundamental to religious understanding. Paul's mirror was dark glass, and he knew how faint were its image and the light it reflected. Words about God offer the same dark perspective, but like imperfect glass they can still show a way out of darkness, beyond our own religious and cultural limits. The vision of God that is opened to us, however shadowed by the private passions of the poet or prophet, can be ours to experience with sympathy or shock, with consolation, surprise, or grief. No one knows God or speaks of God apart from experience, and our experiences are all different—and all limited. But the finitude of experience gives it intensity and urges us forward in awareness that the mystery beyond us is somehow penetrable and that even darkness has its revelatory power.

Only through representation can we speak of God. The mystery of language, its origins, its capacity to separate us from the nonhuman, its existence outside time and space leads us to what is beyond all human signs and all human words. Language expresses the transcendent; it always points to what is beyond direct experience. Poetic language, especially, points beyond itself and beyond private experience to what is both universal and newly recognizable. Poetic language takes us sometimes into the darkness of human experience in which we cry out for meaning, but it is what we call God that makes meaning possible. Without the transcendent, we are imprisoned in an endless chain of words connected only to one another. The possibility of a Presence beyond language can give purpose to language and meaning even to the experience of absence. This collection of poems is a small contribution to the struggle for meaning and the search for what our theologies cannot enclose.

"God," for the purpose of this anthology of poetry, is the one God of the Hebrew Bible or the God acknowledged by men and women in monotheistic cultures. This definition includes the Christian understanding of God as the First Person of the Trinity, or the one described in both Hebrew and Christian Scripture as "the God of Abraham, Isaac, and Jacob." That same deity is worshiped by Muslims for whom "There is no God but God," "the Lord of all, the merciful Lord." That so many poets, believers and unbelievers alike, have speculated about this Being, this hidden, incomprehensible, but fascinating Mystery, urges a gathering of words—a congregation of psalmists and hymnmakers, singers, poets, prophets, and rebels who can function as a chorus of voices questioning and celebrating. The particular chorus that constitutes this anthology is not always in harmony, but discord, like darkness, offers contrasting pleasure.

Other than selected scriptural passages that have become part of the Western religious tradition and a few brief selections that have taken on in translation a life of their own, this anthology includes only poems originally written in English. The justly famous King James Version of the Bible has inspired much of the diction and prosody of religious poetry in English; however, the scriptural passages here are from, and the notes throughout are based on, the New Revised Standard Version, which is more accessible to contemporary readers and more grounded in contemporary biblical scholarship.

Poems for this anthology have been generally selected on the basis of their recognized excellence and the reputation of the poet. It is interesting that in some instances a poet's observations about God may be less well known than his or her other published work. In addition, several poems have been included that are especially important in religious tradition. Like favorite scriptural passages, they have become part of the vocabulary of belief. To read them again is to acknowledge their significance in cultural memory and their relationship to contemporary religious expression.

To reflect on the history of worship requires acknowledging the hymns that have helped to bring emotion to that worship, coloring it with familiarity and the assurance of security. The earliest sung versions of the Psalms and the later spirituals of an oppressed people awaken memories of hope in times of suffering. These lyrics still evoke the energy and faith that inspired them, and they continue to inspire beyond their cultural origins. Gospel music, which emerged in the 1920s and became popular within a decade, drew its inspiration not only from revivalist prayer meetings but also from blues, jazz, circus songs, and dance. Religious lyrics blended with urban culture, generating language that has permeated the churches and prayers of people who never lived in the original settings of these songs, who never heard the great performers and singers who made them a vital part of American culture.

The poems collected here are grouped into three sections. In the first, God is imagined as speaking. The word of God is always a human word; there is, after all, no divine language, except for what in Christian thought is the Word of God, the Son. Here we use "Word of God" in its lesser sense: the words that try to speak of God, that assert in their assumed voice that God does speak, somehow, some way, to the created world. Scripture constitutes for the believer a special instance of that spoken word. This anthology does not challenge that assumption, but it acknowledges that the scriptural word, however inspired, is yet mediated. The prophets and the sages were men (and perhaps women) of their time guided by the Lord who spoke, but their own language was specific to a culture and a moment in history. That we continue to draw inspiration from their words is evidence of the depth and power of their vision.

The second section of the anthology groups poems that can properly be referred to as prayers. The poet's stated audience is

God. Like St. Augustine of Hippo, who dictated his *Confessions* to a scribe because he wanted his words to God to be heard by others, the poet publishes his prayers. Like prophets who also urged that their words be written down and preserved, poets write for others to read. Belief in God is never exclusively private, and we share our religious experience so that we ourselves can understand it better. We tell our stories, call out our prayers, listen to those of others, and create in history a community of seekers.

The third section is a collection of poems that speak *of* God—not always favorably and not always predictably, yet with images and lyrics that stir and startle the imagination. That quality of poetry is its reason for being. The God of believers is, after all, the one who makes all things new; words that speak of God must open the possibility of newness and life. Poetry helps us see beyond our customary (and comfortable) perspective. Therefore, "poem" is the word I have adopted to describe the offerings in this section, rather than "Word" or "Prayer," because God is neither the speaker nor the inscribed audience.

Poets who speak to and about God disclose their own creedal assumptions, but their words give new insights. Scripture itself testifies to a range of theologies that can all be considered inspired. One prophet's inspiration does not necessarily agree with another's. Careful study of scriptural texts discloses the struggle of Hebrew believers to come to terms with the God they believed was theirs to trust and to proclaim to the nations, the God they called by different names but whose revealed name they dared not pronounce. The writer of Deuteronomy announces that God will punish the disobedient down to their children and their children's children to the fourth generation. Ezekiel argues that each person will answer for his or her own sins, that the children of the disobedient will not suffer for the sins of their ancestors. To the theology of the Deuteronomist, the author of Job responds that suffering is not a punishment from God, whose ways are beyond human questions. The writer of Ecclesiastes

(Qoheleth in Hebrew) comes as close to skepticism as biblical inspiration can tolerate, and the tone of that text is remarkably close to Thomas Hardy's brooding preoccupations. The world of the Bible often looks very much like our own.

Conflicting ideas of the godhead testify to the limitations of history and of human understanding, but the range of religious speculation opens an infinite horizon of possibilities. For the late Wisdom writers of Hebrew Scripture, God is unknown and inaccessible. For those secure in their theologies, God is always present, always caring, always the mysterious lover of each believer, the eternal seeker of each nonbeliever. This is the God of Jones Very, of Edward Taylor, of George Herbert and Francis Thompson. For others, less convinced but equally passionate, God's ways cannot be measured so clearly. "The look of Thee, what is it like?" asks Emily Dickinson. "Why was I born?" asks Job. " What awful brain compels His awful hand?" says Countee Cullen, whose query is the underside of the psalmist's question and of Gerard Manley Hopkins's complaint: "Why do sinners' ways prosper?"

Each theistic religious tradition offers a vision, but adherents do not always see the same God or experience the same divine presence. The medieval audience of *Noye's Fludde* heard a cheery God who regarded Noah finally as his "darling deare," an affectionate address that must have modified their understanding of divine justice. Emily Dickinson did not embrace fully her Congregationalist heritage. Milton did not accept all the tenets of Puritanism; Gerard Manley Hopkins became not just Roman Catholic but a Jesuit priest, embracing a spirituality that urged him to discern the smallest parts of the material world and to see in them their inner nature and the unity of all creation. John Henry Newman converted to the Church he once resisted.

Within each tradition, and sometimes across traditions, various spiritualities emerge. It would be hard to imagine the great African American hymns apart from the horrors of slavery that generated despair, hope, longing, and faith in the God that led the Hebrews out of Egypt. These songs have crossed over into a world heritage and can be heard in the churches that once excluded their composers and singers; and the songs of the children of slaves have been mingled with the songs of protest. Thus rituals are given new life.

The prayer forms we experience or do not experience as children and use as adults shape and express our sense of God. But the language of ritual, like the language of our parents and the customs of the past, arouses both devotion and resistance. Alicia Ostriker alludes to Abraham's "memorable logo," "a mark of absolute distinction," ordered by the God who would not permit Abraham to discuss the divine plans with his wife. Edward Taylor, inspired by the Lord's Supper ritually observed, composed hundreds of meditations. George Herbert's sense of God's presence culminates in the meal: "And I did sit and eat."

Poetry about God is often deeply personal, and rituals are familiar in the root sense of that word. But when cultural and political conditions press upon the sense of the divine or belief in God motivates reflection on social conditions, the poem itself moves to concerns other than private devotion and familial customs. Alexander Pope rather approves of the Great Chain of Being. "Whatever is, is right," he once argued. To worship what cannot be changed, however, is to worship oppression. "Mercy has a human heart," writes William Blake, "pity a human face," and later, "Can I see another's woe / And not be in sorrow too?" The sense that we can pity even God urges the pastor in a Gwendolyn Brooks poem to muse "Who walks with Him, dares to take his arm?"

The God of tradition and ritual can and should be interrogated, and that imperative throws open yet more interesting possibilities. Marilyn Nelson's "Mama" is one of the more vivid. The God of *Mama's Promises* is black and female: "I want to be remembered / with big bare arms akimbo . . . with breasts that never look empty." If the God of empire and tribal preference is out of favor, so too is the male God speaking exclusively to men. Who is to say that God is not our mother? Women of every color know who it is that nurtures and who should have been consulted when Isaac's life was on the line. Their conversations with God offer a whole new understanding of tradition.

Each generation, each people has its vision. Can any of them give us all there is to see? " All things change / when you measure them," writes Kathleen Norris. "You might as well sing, the sound of your voice joining the others, like waters overflowing / the name of the living God."

Like waters overflowing, poets give us to drink. The doubters, believers, lovers, and philosophers, the anguished and flippant, submissive and prayerful, speak for us and about us.

Through their words, we may possibly see God anew.

INVISIBLE LIGHT

PART ONE

From God: The Word

I am the first and I am the last;
   besides me there is no god.
Who is like me? Let them proclaim it,
   let them declare and set it forth before me.
Who has announced from of old the things to come?
   Let them tell us what is yet to be.
Do not fear, or be afraid;
   have I not told you from of old and declared it?
   You are my witnesses!
Is there any god besides me?
   There is no other rock; I know not one.

—CHAPTER 44:6–8

THE PROPHET known as Second Isaiah lived in Babylon toward the end of the captivity (587–539 B.C.E.). The imminent release of the Jewish people from their forced exile inspired this unknown writer to compose "The Book of the Consolation of Israel," chapters 40–55 of the Book of the Prophet Isaiah. This important section of a dialogue between Israel and God, composed as a legal argument, is one of the first unambiguous declarations of monotheism in Jewish literature. The God of Israel is the only God, says the composer of these songs. There is no other.

"Hear, O my people, and I will speak,
   O Israel, I will testify against you.
  I am God, your God.
Not for your sacrifices do I rebuke you;
   your burnt offerings are continually before me.
I will not accept a bull from your house,
  or goats from your folds.
For every wild animal of the forest is mine,
   the cattle on a thousand hills.
I know all the birds of the air,
   and all that moves in the field is mine.

"If I were hungry, I would not tell you,
   for the world and all that is in it is mine.
Do I eat the flesh of bulls,
  or drink the blood of goats?
Offer to God a sacrifice of thanksgiving,
  and pay your vows to the Most High.
Call on me in the day of trouble;
   I will deliver you, and you shall glorify me."

But to the wicked God says:
   "What right have you to recite my statutes,
   or take my covenant on your lips?
For you hate discipline,
   and you cast my words behind you.
You make friends with a thief when you see one,
   and you keep company with adulterers.

"You give your mouth free rein for evil
  and your tongue frames deceit.
You sit and speak against your kin;
  you slander your own mother's child.
These things you have done and I have been silent;
  you thought that I was one just like yourself.
But now I rebuke you, and lay the charge before you."

—vv. 7–21

THIS PSALM may have been composed for a covenant-renewal litur-
gy, such as the Feast of Tabernacles. The imagery is of God the Lord
(overlord) summoning Israel, the vassal, to account. Sacrifices and the
sacrificial system are not condemned, but the essential sacrifice is that
of praise and thanksgiving. Sacrifices do not coerce God, who does
not need them.

Then the Lord answered Job out of the whirlwind:
"Who is this that darkens counsel by words without
    knowledge?
Gird up your loins like a man,
    I will question you, and you shall declare to me.

"Where were you when I laid the foundations of the earth?
Tell me, if you have understanding.
Who determined its measurements—
    surely you know!
    Or who stretched the line upon it?
On what were its bases sunk,
    or who laid its cornerstone
when the morning stars sang together
    and all the heavenly beings shouted for joy?

"Or who shut in the sea with doors,
    when it burst out from the womb?—
when I made the clouds its garment,
    and thick darkness its swaddling band,
and prescribed bounds for it,
    and set bars and doors,
and said, 'Thus far shall you come, and no farther,
    and here shall your proud waves be stopped'?

"Have you commanded the morning since your days began,
    and caused the dawn to know its place,
so that it might take hold of the skirts of the earth,
and the wicked be shaken out of it?

It is changed like clay under the seal,
  and it is dyed like a garment.
Light is withheld from the wicked,
  and their uplifted arm is broken.

"Have you entered into the springs of the sea,
  or walked in the recesses of the deep?
Have the gates of death been revealed to you,
  or have you seen the gates of deep darkness?
Have you comprehended the expanse of the earth?
  Declare, if you know all this."

— CHAPTER 38:1–18

THESE STANZAS introduce the God of the Whirlwind, the Tempest out of which Job hears the voice of the One to whom he complained that he did not deserve the suffering heaped on him. The "patient" Job had argued valiantly to his religious comforters that God had no reason to punish him, that others committed crimes and deserved punishment, but his own ethical behavior could pass rigorous scrutiny. Who was this God who could not be found and whose ways were hidden? Why should God not explain himself? In chapters 38:1–41:34, God responds. The text, classified as wisdom literature, dates from the third century B.C.E. The author is unknown.

GOD

Noye, to me thou arte full able,

And thy sacrifice acceptable,

For I have founde thee true and stable;

On thee nowe muste I myne [think];

Warrye [curse] eairth I will noe more

For mannes synnes that greves me sore,

For of youth mon [man] full yore

   Has bene inclynde to synne.

You shall nowe growe and multiplye,

And eairth againe to edifye,

  . . . .

Of cleane beastes nowe lesse and more

   I give you leve to eate;

Save bloode and fleshe, bouth in feare

Of rouge dead carrion that is heare,

Eate not of that in noe manere,

   For that aye you shall lete [abstain].

Man-slaughter also you shall flee,

For that is not pleasante unto me;

The that sheedeth blood, he or shee,

   Oughte-wher amonge mankinde,

That bloode fowle shedde shalbe

And vengeance have, that men shall see;

Therfore beware now all ye,

   You falle not into that synne.

A forward [covenant], Noye, with thee I make,

And all thy seede, for thy sake,

Of suche vengeance for to slake,

For nowe I have my will;
Heare I behette thee a heste [promise]
That man, woman, fowlde, ney beste,
With watter, while this worlde shall leste,
    I will noe more spill.
My bowe betweyne you and me
In the firmamente shalbe,
By verey tocken that you shall see,
    That suche vengeance shall cease,
That man ne woman shall never more
Be wasted with watter, as hath before;
But for synne that greveth me sore,
    Therfore this vengeance was.
Wher cloudes in the welckine bene,
That ilke [each] bowe shalbe seene,
In tocken that my wrath and teene [sorrow]
    Shall never thus wrocken [wreaked] be.
The stringe is torned towardes you,
And towarde me is bente the bowe,
That suche weither shall never shewe,
    And this behighte [promise] I thee.
My blessinge, Noye, I geve thee heare,
To thee, Noye, my servante deare;
For vengeance shall noe more appeare,
    And nowe fare well, my darlinge deare.

—LL. 269–278, 287–328

FROM THE early fourteenth century to the sixteenth century, a principal form of entertainment in England was the miracle play. Scenes from Hebrew and Christian Scripture were dramatized by local guilds for the edification and instruction of Christian believers. These plays were eventually grouped into cycles, the most well known being the York, Chester, and Wakefield cycles. *Noah's Flood* is part of the Chester cycle. There are five manuscripts of the medieval *Noye's Fludde*. The text here is drawn primarily from the 1592 version, edited by Alfred W. Pollard. Translations have been inserted. The biblical story can be found in Genesis, chapters 6–9.

JOSUAH SYLVESTER

from "Eden," The First Part of the First Day of the II. Week

Adam, quoth He, the beauties manifold
That in this Eden thou dost heer behold,
Are all thine; onely enter; (sacred Race)
Come, take possession of this wealthy place,
The Earth's sole glory: take (dear Son) to thee
This Farm's demains, leave the Chief right to me;
And th' onely Rent that of it I reserve, is
One Tree's fair fruit, to shew thy sute and service:
Be thou the Liege, and I Lord Paramount,
Ile not exact hard fines (as men shall woont).
For signe of Homage, and for seal of Faith,
Of all the Profits this Possession hath,
I onely ask one Tree; whose fruit I will
For Sacrament shall stand of *Good* and *Ill*.
Take all the rest, I bid thee; but I vow
By th' un-named Name, where-to all knees do bow,
And by the keen Darts of my kindled ire
(More fiercely burning than consuming fire)
That of the fruit of *Knowledge* if thou feed,
Death, dreadfull death, shal plague thee and thy seed.
If then, the happy state thou holdst of me,
My holy mildnesse, nor high Majestie,

If faith nor honour curb thy bold ambition,
Yet weigh thy selfe, and thine own Seeds condition.

—LL. 452–475

IN THE sixteenth century, the period of the great English translations of the Bible, other religious works were also translated from Latin, French, and Anglo-Saxon. One of the most popular religious texts was the epic of Guillaume du Bartas (*Divine Weekes and Workes*), translated by Josuah Sylvester into heroic couplets. The epic is divided into weeks, the weeks into days. The epic recapitulates biblical accounts in Genesis.

The Pulley

GEORGE HERBERT

When God at first made man,
Having a glass of blessings standing by,
"Let us" (said He) "pour on him all we can;
Let the world's riches, which dispersèd lie,
   Contract into a span."

So strength first made a way;
Then beauty flow'd, then wisdom, honor, pleasure;
When almost all was out, God made a stay,
Perceiving that alone of all his treasure
   Rest in the bottom lay.

"For if I should" (said He)
"Bestow this jewel also on my creature,
He would adore my gifts instead of me,
And rest in nature, not the God of nature:
   So both should losers be.

"Yet let him keep the rest,
But keep them with repining restlessness;
Let him be rich and weary, that at least,
If goodness lead him not, yet weariness
   May toss him to my breast."

For Man will hearken to his glozing lies,
And easily transgress the sole Command,
Sole pledge of his obedience: So will fall
Hee and his faithless Progeny: whose fault?
Whose but his own? ingrate, he had of mee
All he could have; I made him just and right,
Sufficient to have stood, though free to fall.
Such I created all th' Ethereal Powers
And Spirits, both them who stood and them who fail'd;
Freely they stood who stood, and fell who fell.
Not free, what proof could they have giv'n sincere
Of true allegiance, constant Faith or Love,
Where only what they needs must do, appear'd,
Not what they would? What praise could they receive?
What pleasure I from such obedience paid,
When Will and Reason (Reason also is choice)
Useless and vain, of freedom both despoil'd,
Made passive both, had serv'd necessity,
Not mee. They therefore as to right belong'd,
So were created, nor can justly accuse
Thir maker or thir making, or thir Fate;
As if Predestination over-rul'd
Thir will, dispos'd by absolute Decree
Or high foreknowledge; they themselves decreed
Thir own revolt, not I; if I foreknew,

Foreknowledge had no influence on their fault,
Which had no less prov'd certain unforeknown.
So without least impulse or shadow of Fate,
Or aught by me immutably foreseen,
They trespass, Authors to themselves in all
Both what they judge and what they choose; for so
I form'd them free, and free they must remain,
Till they enthrall themselves: I else must change
Thir nature, and revoke the high Decree
Unchangeable, Eternal, which ordain'd
Thir freedom: they themselves ordain'd thir fall.
The first sort by thir own suggestion fell,
Self-tempted, self deprav'd: Man falls deceiv'd
By th' other first: Man therefore shall find grace,
The other none: in Mercy and Justice both,
Through Heav'n and Earth, so shall my glory excel,
But Mercy first and last shall brightest shine.

—LL. 93–134

THIS SPEECH in Book 3 of *Paradise Lost* represents God speaking to the Son and describes the flight of Satan to the newly created world, where he will attempt to destroy the human beings God has placed there. God knows that, because of Satan's influence, they also will revolt. Milton argues that God's foreknowledge of their failure is not an indication of their predestination; humanity is free, but easily tempted. According to the argument, therefore, Adam and his progeny will find mercy and grace.

The Future Peace and Glory of the Church

Isaiah LX. 15–20

WILLIAM COWPER

Hear what God the Lord hath spoken:—
O my people, faint and few;
Comfortless, afflicted, broken,
Fair abodes I build for you:
Thorns of heart-felt tribulation
Shall no more perplex your ways;
You shall name your walls, Salvation,
And your gates shall all be Praise.
There, like streams that feed the garden,
Pleasures, without end, shall flow;
For the LORD, your faith rewarding,
All his bounty shall bestow:
Still in undisturb'd possession,
Peace and righteousness shall reign;
Never shall you feel oppression,
Hear the voice of war again.
You no more your suns descending,
Waning moons no more shall see;
But, your griefs for ever ending,
Find eternal noon in me:
GOD shall rise, and shining o'er ye,
Change to day the gloom of night;
He, the LORD, shall be your glory,
God your everlasting light.

WILLIAM COWPER suffered from frequent bouts of severe mental illness. Living in Olney, he was comforted by the local vicar, who encouraged him to collaborate in composing hymns. The more than 300 hymns he composed were published in 1779 as *The Olney Hymns*. This is hymn 10.

The passage from Isaiah on which this hymn is based was written at the end of the Babylonian exile, when it became clear that Cyrus, the Persian ruler, would release the Jews and allow them to return to Jerusalem. Chapter 40 introduces the text known as Second Isaiah (or Deutero-Isaiah) and sometimes called "The Book of the Consolation of Israel."

My Meat and Drink

I do not need thy food, but thou dost mine;
For this will but the body's wants repair,
And soon again for meat like this 'twill pine,
And so be fed by thee with daily care;
But that which I can give thou needs but eat,
And thou shalt find it in thyself to be;
Forever formed within a living meat,
On which to feed will make thy spirit free;
Thou shalt not hunger more, for freely given
The bread on which the spirit daily feeds;
This is the bread that cometh down from heaven,
Of which who eats no other food he needs;
But this doth grow within him day by day,
Increasing more the more he takes away.

LINE 11: In Exodus 16:4, God gives bread to the Israelites as they travel in the desert: "Then the Lord said to Moses, 'I am going to rain bread from heaven for you.'" The image recurs in John 6:33: "For the bread of God is that which comes down from heaven and gives life to the world." In John's gospel, the bread from heaven is the Word of God.

There is naught for thee by thy haste to gain;
'Tis not the swift with Me that win the race;
Through long endurance of delaying pain,
Thine opened eye shall see thy Father's face;
Nor here nor there, where now thy feet would turn,
Thou wilt find Him who ever seeks for thee;
But let obedience quench desires that burn,
And where thou art, thy Father too will be.
Behold! as day by day the spirit grows,
Thou see'st by inward light things hid before;
Till what God is, thyself, his image, shows;
And thou dost wear the robe that first thou wore,
When bright with radiance from His forming hand,
He saw thee Lord of all his Creatures stand.

LINE 2: Cf. Ecclesiastes 9:11: "under the sun the race is not to the swift, nor the battle to the strong."

Boston Hymn

RALPH WALDO EMERSON

(Read in Music Hall, January 1, 1863)

The word of the Lord by night
To the watching Pilgrims came,
As they sat by the seaside,
And filled their hearts with flame.

God said, I am tired of kings,
I suffer them no more;
Up to my ear the morning brings
The outrage of the poor.

Think ye I made this ball
A field of havoc and war,
Where tyrants great and tyrants small
Might harry the weak and poor?

My angel,—his name is Freedom,—
Choose him to be your king;
He shall cut pathways east and west,
And fend you with his wing.

Lo! I uncover the land
Which I hid of old time in the West,
As the sculptor uncovers the statue
When he has wrought his best;

I show Columbia, of the rocks
Which dip their foot in the seas
And soar to the airborne flocks
Of clouds and the boreal fleece.

I will divide my goods;
Call in the wretch and slave:

None shall rule but the humble.
And none but Toil shall have.

I will never have a noble,
No lineage counted great;
Fishers and choppers and ploughmen
Shall constitute a state.

Go, cut down trees in the forest
And trim the straightest boughs;
Cut down trees in the forest
And build me a wooden house.

Call the people together,
The young men and the sires,
The digger in the harvest field,
Hireling, and him that hires;

And here in a pine state-house
They shall choose men to rule
In every needful faculty,
In church, and state, and school.

Lo, now! if these poor men
Can govern the land and sea
And make just laws below the sun,
As planets faithful be.

And ye shall succor men;
'Tis nobleness to serve;
Help them who cannot help again:
Beware from right to swerve.

I break your bonds and masterships,
And I unchain the slave:
Free be his heart and hand henceforth
As wind and wandering wave.

I cause from every creature
His proper good to flow:
As much as he is and doeth,
So much he shall bestow.

But, laying hands on another
To coin his labor and sweat,
He goes in pawn to his victim
For eternal years in debt.

To-day unbind the captive
So only are ye unbound;
Lift up a people from the dust,
Trump of their rescue, sound!

Pay ransom to the owner,
And fill the bag to the brim.
Who is the owner? The slave is owner,
And ever was. Pay him.

O North! give him beauty for rags,
And honor, O South! for his shame;
Nevada! coin thy golden crags
With Freedom's image and name.

Up! and the dusky race
That sat in darkness long—
Be swift their feet as antelopes,
And as behemoth strong.

Come, East and West and North,
By races, as snowflakes,
And carry my purpose forth,
Which neither halts nor shakes.

My will fulfilled shall be,
For, in daylight or in dark,
My thunderbolt has eyes to see
His way home to the mark.

LONG AFTER Emerson resigned his Unitarian ministry, he remained committed to the rhetoric of religion. Linking God not to the churches he dismissed as ossified but to his political convictions, he preached a secular faith in self-reliance and freedom.

The Island

R. S. Thomas

And God said, I will build a church here
And cause this people to worship me,
And afflict them with poverty and sickness
In return for centuries of hard work
And patience. And its walls shall be hard as
Their hearts, and its windows let in the light
Grudgingly, as their minds do, and the priest's words
   be drowned
By the wind's caterwauling. All this I will do,

Said God, and watch the bitterness in their eyes
Grow, and their lips suppurate with
Their prayers. And their women shall bring forth
On my altars, and I will choose the best
Of them to be thrown back into the sea.
And that was only on one island.

IN HIS own introduction to an anthology of religious poetry, R. S.
Thomas distinguished the poet from the mystic by suggesting that to
the mystic the *Deus absconditus* is immediate; to the poet he is mediated.
In *H'm*, from which this selection is taken, the poet translates the hid-
denness of God into the mystery of suffering. See also his "Via Nega-
tiva," from the same collection, in the third section of this anthology.

The Story of Abraham

ALICIA OSTRIKER

I started by reading the banner headline
The way you read the big print at the eye doctor's.
It said I AM THE LORD GOD
ALMIGHTY AND I LOVE YOU
ESPECIALLY.
No problem. Very good.
One line down it said PACK UP,
I'M SENDING YOU OVERSEAS. It said
YOU WILL HAVE AS MANY CHILDREN
AS THERE ARE SANDS IN THE SEA
AND STARS IN THE SKY.
THEY WILL POSSESS THE LAND AND
I AM PERSONALLY GOING TO BLESS THEM.
The smaller print said: I am going
To bless them as long as they obey me.
Otherwise there may be
Certain repercussions. The even smaller
Print explained how we needed
A memorable logo for our organization
And he had just the ticket, a mark of absolute
Distinction, it would only hurt for a minute.
The print kept getting smaller and blurrier,
The instructions more bizarre.
Hold on, I interrupted. I'd like to check
Some of this out with my wife.
NO WAY. THIS IS BETWEEN US MEN.
AND IF YOU HAPPEN TO BE THINKING
ABOUT LOOPHOLES

FORGET IT. It said they preferred
Not to use strongarm techniques. It said
BEAR IN MIND, FRIEND,
YOU'VE ALREADY SIGNED ON.

THE STORY of Abraham begins at Genesis 12. In Genesis 17:10–11, cir-
cumcision is described as the sign of the covenant between God and
the descendants of Abraham.

PAUL MURRAY

Smaller than the small
I am that still centre
within you
that needle's eye
through which all the threads
of the universe are drawn.

Perhaps you think you know me
but you do not know me.

Of everything that is,
of every word that is spoken
on the lips
or in the heart,
of every thought and hope and wish,
I am the silent witness.

Nearer to you than ecstasy
in the blood
yet more mysterious far

I am the guardian of every colour
that catches the eye,
of every taste
that pleases the tongue,
of every word
that speaks to the heart.

Perhaps you think you know me
but you do not know me.

Mine is the voice
that sings out of the voiceless
night, that rises
like music out of the root
of the dark thorn, out of the lucid
throat of the fountain.

Smaller than the small

I am the seed
of all that is known
and unknown.

I am the root
and stem of meaning,
the ground

of wonder. Through me,
each leading
tendril of desire
is drawn,
and breathes in
consciousness of Being.

And yet when you open
your ears to my voice
and listen with all your hearing
and listen again,
no subtle joining of notes and words,
no vertical song is heard

but silence is singing.

And when you open your eyes
to my appearance
but cannot see me,
or when you close your eyes
and close your ears in concentration

and look with your hands
and turn back again the pages
of sleep's dark scripture,
no great or terrible sign awakes,
no vision burns

but absence is shining.

Mine is the secret
that lies hidden
like the lustrous pearl

gleaming
within its oyster

the deepest secret
the secret
hidden within the secret.

THE EPIGRAPH to the volume of poems from which this has been se-
lected is from Simone Weil: "The apparent absence of God in this
world is the actual reality of God."

I want to be remembered
with big bare arms akimbo
and feet splay-toed and flat arched
on the welcome mat of dirt.

I want to be remembered
as a voice that was made to be singing
the lullaby of shadows
as a child fades into a dream.

I want to be as familiar
as the woman in the background
when the heroine is packing
and the Yankee soldiers come.

Hair covered with a bandanna,
I want to be remembered
as an autumn under maples:
a show of incredible leaves.

I want to be remembered
with breasts that never look empty,
with a child-bearing generous waistline
and with generous, love-making hips.

I want to be remembered
with a dark face absorbing all colors
and giving them back twice as brightly,
like water remembering light.

I want to be remembered
with a simple name, like Mama:

as an open door from creation,
as a picture of someone you know.

MAMA'S PROMISES, the sequence of poems from which this selection is taken, draws from domestic imagery and experience a picture of God as the narrator's caring, humming, sometimes angry, always nourishing, loving mother.

PART TWO

To God: The Prayer

O Lord, our Sovereign,
   how majestic is your name in all the earth!
You have set your glory above the heavens.
   Out of the mouths of babes and infants
you have founded a bulwark because of your foes
   to silence the enemy and the avenger.

When I look at your heavens, the work of your fingers,
   the moon and the stars that you have established;
what are human beings that you are mindful of them,
   mortals that you care for them?

Yet you have made them a little lower than God,
   and crowned them with glory and honor.
You have given them dominion over the works of your hands;
   you have put all things under their feet,
all sheep and oxen,
   and also the beasts of the field, the birds of the air, and the
   fish of the sea,
whatever passes along the paths of the seas.

O Lord, our Sovereign,
   how majestic is your name in all the earth!

PSALM 8 is classified as a "hymn of praise," to distinguish it from a personal or collective lament, a thanksgiving psalm, or a psalm expressive of classical wisdom theology. Composed over a period of almost seven hundred years (1000–300 B.C.E.) and popularly attributed to David, the Psalms are liturgical expressions of faith in God, sometimes addressed as Elohim (Psalms 42–83), but usually as Adonai or Yahweh. Psalm 8 begins "O Yahweh, our Adonai" ("O Lord, our Lord"). In line 6 of Psalm 8, the word *Elohim* is variously translated as *angels*, *gods*, or *a god*.

The Knight's Prayer

ANONYMOUS

God be in my head
And in my understanding;
God be in mine eyes
    And in my looking;
God be in my mouth
    And in my speaking;
God be in my heart
    And in my thinking;
God be at my end,
    And at my departing.

—SIXTEENTH CENTURY

A Prayer

SIR THOMAS MORE

Grant, I thee pray, such heat into mine heart
That to this love of thine may be equàl;
Grant me from Satan's service to astart,
With whom me rueth so long to have been thrall;
Grant me, good Lord and Creator of all,
The flame to quench of all sinful desire
And in thy love set all mine heart afire.
That when the journey of this deadly life
My silly ghost hath finishèd, and thence
Departen must without his fleshly wife,
Alone into his Lordès high presènce,
He may thee find, O well of indulgènce,
In thy lordship not as a lord, but rather
As a very tender, loving father.

JOSUAH SYLVESTER

Alpha and Omega, God alone:
  Eloi, My God, the Holy-One;
Whose power is Omnipotence:
Whose Wisedome is Omni-science:
Whose Beeing is All Soveraigne Blisse:
Whose Worke Perfection's Fulnesse is:
  Under All things, not under-cast;
Over All things, not over-plac't:
Within All things, not there included;
Without All things, not thence excluded:
  Above All, over All things raigning;
Beneath All, All things aye sustayning:
Without All, All conteyning sole:
Within All, filling-full the Whole:
  Within All, no where comprehended;
Without All, no where more extended;
Under, by nothing over-topped:
Over, by nothing under-propped:

Unmov'd, Thou movs't the World about;
Unplac't, Within it, or Without:
Unchanged, time-lesse, Time Thou changest:
Th'unstable, Thou, still stable, rangest;
No outward Force, nor inward Fate,
Can Thy drad Essence alterate:
To-day, To-morrow, yester-day
With Thee, are One, and instant aye;
Aye undivided, ended never:
To-day, with Thee, indures for-ever.

Thou, Father, mad'st this mighty Ball:
Of nothing thou created'st All,
After th' *Idea* of thy Minde,
Conferring Forme to every kinde.

Thou wert, Thou art, Thou wilt be ever:
And Thine *Elect*, rejectest never.

"THE FATHER" is the first of a three-part poem entitled "The Mysterie of Mysteries." Parts 2 and 3 are "The Sonne" and "The Holy Ghost."

Line 1: Alpha and omega are the first and last letters of the Greek alphabet. God in Revelation 1:8 and 21:6 is called "the Alpha and the Omega." In Isaiah 44:6, God says, "I am the first and I am the last."

Line 2: *Eloi* is an Aramaic variant of the Hebrew *Eli*. In Mark 15:34 Jesus uses this word to address God.

De Profundis

THOMAS CAMPION

Out of my soul's depth to thee my cries have sounded:
Let thine ears my plaints receive, on just fear grounded.
Lord, should'st thou weigh our faults, who's not confounded?

But with grace thou censur'st thine when they have errèd,
Therefore shall thy blessed name be loved and fearèd.
Ev'n to thy throne my thoughts and eyes are rearèd.
Thee alone my hopes attend, on thee relying;
In thy sacred word I'll trust, to thee fast flying,
Long ere the watch shall break, the morn descrying.

In the mercies of our God who live securèd,
May of full redemption rest in him assurèd,
Their sin-sick souls by him shall be recurèd.

THE TITLE and the poem are based on Psalm 130, which begins, "Out of the depths I cry to you, O Lord."

THOMAS CAMPION

Author of light, revive my dying spright;
Redeem it from the snares of all-confounding night.
       Lord, light me to thy blessed way:
For, blind with worldly vain desires, I wander as a stray.
    Sun and moon, stars and underlights I see,
But all their glorious beams are mists and darkness, being
    compared to thee.

Fountain of health, my soul's deep wounds recure,
Sweet showers of pity rain, wash my uncleanness pure.
       One drop of thy desired grace
The faint and fading heart can raise, and in joy's bosom place.
    Sin and death, hell and tempting fiends may rage;
But God his own will guard, and their sharp pains and grief
    in time assuage.

JOHN DONNE

Thou hast made me, and shall thy work decay?
Repair me now, for now mine end doth haste;
I run to death, and death meets me as fast,
And all my pleasures are like yesterday;
I dare not move my dim eyes any way,
Despair behind, and death before doth cast
Such terror, and my feebled flesh doth waste
By sin in it, which it towards hell doth weigh;
Only Thou art above, and when towards Thee
By Thy leave I can look, I rise again;
But our old subtle foe so tempteth me
That not one hour I can myself sustain;
Thy grace may wing me to prevent his art,
And Thou like adamant draw mine iron heart.

JOHN DONNE

Batter my heart, three-personed God; for You
As yet but knock, breathe, shine, and seek to mend;
That I may rise, and stand, o'erthrow me, and bend
Your force, to break, blow, burn, and make me new.
I, like an usurped town, to another due,
Labor to admit You, but oh, to no end!
Reason, Your viceroy in me, me should defend,
But is captived, and proves weak or untrue,
Yet dearly I love You, and would be loved fain,
But am betrothed unto Your enemy:
Divorce me, untie, or break that knot again,
Take me to You, imprison me, for I
Except You enthral me, never shall be free,
Nor ever chaste, except You ravish me.

IN THE Sir Herbert Grierson edition of the Holy Sonnets, this is sonnet 14. In Helen Gardner's *The Divine Poems*, this is sonnet 10.

A Hymn to God the Father

JOHN DONNE

Wilt Thou forgive that sin where I begun,
   Which is my sin, though it were done before?
Wilt Thou forgive those sins through which I run,
   And do run still, though still I do deplore?
   When Thou hast done, thou hast not done,
      For I have more.

Wilt Thou forgive that sin which I have won
   Others to sin? and made my sin their door?
Wilt Thou forgive that sin which I did shun
   A year or two, but wallowed in a score?
   When thou hast done, thou hast not done,
      For I have more.

I have a sin of fear, that when I have spun
   My last thread, I shall perish on the shore;
Swear by Thyself that at my death thy Sun
   Shall shine as it shines now, and heretofore;
   And having done that, Thou hast done.
      I have no more.

THIS HYMN was probably written when Donne was gravely ill in
1623. "Swear by Thyself" in line 15 alludes to Genesis 22:16: "By myself
I have sworn, says the Lord," and Hebrews 6:13–18, in which God
shows "even more clearly to the heirs of the promise the unchangeable
character of his purpose," swearing by himself. In the 1633 edition of
Donne's poems, several variants appear: "is" in line 2 is "was"; "those
sins" in line 3 is "that sin"; "Sun" in line 15 is "Son"; "it" in line 16 is
"he"; "have" in line 18 is "fear."

To Heaven

BEN JONSON

Good and great God, can I not think of thee
    But it must, straight, my melancholy be?
Is it interpreted in me disease
    That, laden with my sins, I seek for ease?
Oh, be thou witness, that the reins dost know
    And hearts of all, if I be sad for show,
And judge me after, if I dare pretend
    To ought but grace, or aim at other end.
As thou art all, so be thou all to me,
    First, midst, and last, converted one, and three;
My faith, my hope, my love, and in this state
    My judge, my witness, and my advocate.
Where have I been this while exiled from thee?
    And whither rapt, now thou but stoop'st to me?
Dwell, dwell here still; oh being everywhere
    How can I doubt to find thee ever, here?
I know my state, both full of shame and scorn,
    Conceived in sin and unto labor born,
Standing with fear, and must with horror fall,
    And destined unto judgment, after all.
I feel my griefs too, and there scarce is ground
    Upon my flesh t'inflict another wound.
Yet dare I not complain, or wish for death
    With holy Paul, lest it be thought the breath
Of discontent, or that these prayers be
    For weariness of life, not love of thee.

LINE 10: "converted one, and three" is an allusion to the Trinity in Christian belief.

Lines 24–25: See Romans 7:24: "Who will rescue me from this body of death?"

A Hymn to God the Father

BEN JONSON

Hear me, O God!
A broken heart
Is my best part:
Use still thy rod
  That I may prove
  Therein thy love.

If thou hadst not
  Been stern to me,
  But left me free,
I had forgot
  Myself and thee.

For sin's so sweet,
  As minds ill bent
  Rarely repent,
Until they meet
  Their punishment.

Who more can crave
  Than thou hast done,
  That gav'st a son
To free a slave,
  First made of nought,
  With all since bought?

Sin, Death, and Hell
    His glorious Name
    Quite overcame,
Yet I rebel,
    And slight the same.

But I'll come in
    Before my loss,
    Me farther toss
As sure to win
    Under his cross.

Man's Natural Infirmity

JOHN DAY

What means my God? Why dost present to me
Such glorious objects? Can a blind man see?
Why dost thou call? Why dost thou beckon so?
Wouldst have me come? Lord, can a cripple go?
Or, why dost thou expect that I should raise
Thy glory with my voice: the dumb can't praise.
Unscale my dusky eyes; then I'll express
Thy glorious object's strong attractiveness:
Dip thou my limbs in thy Bethesda's lake—
I'll scorn my earthly crutches; I'll forsake
Myself: touch thou my tongue, and then I'll sing
An hallelujah to my glorious King:
Raise me from this grave—then I shall be
Alive, and I'll bestow my life on thee.
Till thou, Elijah-like, dost overspread
My limbs, I'm blind, I'm lame, I'm dumb—I'm
　　　　dead!

LINE 9: "Bethesda's lake": See John 5:2. The reference is to the orig-
inal Hebrew name of the pool near the Sheep Gate in Jerusalem where
the sick gathered to seek healing. According to pious tradition, the
first person to enter the pool after an angel stirred the waters would be
healed. Jesus is described as healing a paralytic there.

Line 10: A possible reference to Isaiah 6:7, in which an angel touch-
es Isaiah's mouth to purify his lips for the task of preaching.

Line 15: "Elijah-like": In 1 Kings 17:21, the prophet Elijah stretches
his body three times over the corpse of a child and prays for the child's
recovery. "The Lord listened to the voice of Elijah; the life of the child
came into him again, and he revived" (1 Kings 17:22).

A Song

RICHARD CRASHAW

Lord, when the sense of Thy sweet grace
Sends up my soul to seek Thy face,
Thy blessed eyes breed such desire
I die in Love's delicious fire.
   O Love, I am Thy sacrifice!
Be still triumphant, blessed eyes!
Still shine on me, fair suns! that I
Still may behold, though still I die.

SECOND PART
   Though still I die, I live again,
Still longing so to be still slain;
So gainful is such loss of breath,
I die even in desire of death.
   Still live in me this loving strife
Of living death and dying life;
For while Thou sweetly slayest me,
Dead to myself, I live in Thee.

THIS POEM may have been inspired by the life and mystical visions of
St. Teresa of Avila, who was canonized in 1622. Crashaw composed
several poems praising her love for God. In "A Hymn to the Name and
Honor of the Admirable Saint Teresa," the poet closes with a similar
reflection: "who in death would live to see / Must learn in life to die
like thee."

The Book

HENRY VAUGHAN

Eternal God! Maker of all
That have lived here since the man's fall;
The Rock of Ages! In whose shade
They live unseen, when here they fade;

Thou knew'st this paper when it was
Mere seed, and after that but grass;
Before 'twas dressed or spun, and when
Made linen, who did wear it then:
What were their lives, their thoughts, and deeds,
Whether good corn or fruitless weeds.

   Thou knew'st this tree when a green shade
Covered it, since a cover made,
And where it flourished, grew and spread,
As if it never should be dead.

   Thou knew'st this harmless beast when he
Did live and feed by Thy decree
On each green thing; then slept—well fed—
Clothed with this skin which now lies spread
A covering o'er this aged book;
Which makes me wisely weep, and look
On my own dust; mere dust it is,
But not so dry and clean as this.
Thou knew'st and saw'st them all, and though
Now scattered thus, dost know them so.

   O knowing, glorious Spirit! When
Thou shalt restore trees, beasts, and men,

When Thou shalt make all new again,
Destroying only death and pain,
Give him amongst Thy works a place
Who in them loved and sought Thy face!

LINE 2: The image of God as a rock—suggestive of strength, protection, and stability—is a constant in Hebrew Scripture. See especially Deuteronomy 32:4, 2 Samuel 22:2, and Psalm 18. Thomas Hastings composed a famous hymn (c. 1830) entitled "Rock of Ages" directed to Christ: "Rock of ages, cleft for me, let me hide myself in thee."

THOMAS TRAHERNE

That all things should be mine,
This makes His bounty most divine,
But that they all more rich should be,
And far more brightly shine,
    As used by me;
It ravishes my soul to see the end,
To which this work so wonderful doth tend.

    That we should make the skies
More glorious far before Thine eyes
Than Thou didst make them, and even Thee
    Far more Thy works to prize,
    As used they be
Than as they're made, is a stupendous work,
Wherein Thy wisdom mightily doth lurk.

    Thy greatness, and Thy love,
    Thy power, in this, my joy doth move;
    Thy goodness and felicity
        In this expressed above
            All praise I see;
While Thy great Godhead over all doth reign,
And such an end in such a sort attain.

    What bound may we assign,
O God, to any work of Thine!
Their endlessness discovers Thee
    In all to be divine;
        A Deity,
That will forevermore exceed the end
Of all that creature's wit can comprehend.

Am I a glorious spring
Of joys and riches to my King?
Are men made Gods? And may they see
　　So wonderful a thing
　　As God in me?
And is my soul a mirror that must shine
Even like the sun and be far more divine?

　　Thy Soul, O God, doth prize
The seas, the earth, our souls, the skies;
As we return the same to Thee
They more delight Thine eyes.
　　And sweeter be
As unto Thee we offer up the same,
Than as to us from Thee at first they came.

　　O how doth Sacred Love
His gifts refine, exalt, improve!
Our love to creatures makes them be
　　In Thine esteem above
　　Themselves to Thee!
O here His goodness evermore admire!
He made our souls to make His creatures higher.

Huswifery

EDWARD TAYLOR

Make me, O Lord, thy Spining Wheele compleate.
  Thy Holy Worde my Distaff make for mee.
Make mine Affections thy Swift Flyers neate
  And make my Soule thy holy Spoole to bee.
  My Conversation make to be thy Reele
  And reele the yarn thereon spun of thy Wheele.

Make me thy Loome then, knit therein this Twine:
  And make thy Holy Spirit, Lord, winde quills:
Then weave the Web thyselfe. The yarn is fine.
  Thine Ordinances make my Fulling Mills.
  Then dy the same in Heavenly Colours Choice,
  All pinkt with Varnisht Flowers of Paradise.

Then cloath therewith mine Understanding, Will,
  Affections, Judgment, Conscience, Memory
My Words, and Actions, that their shine may fill
  My wayes with glory and thee glorify.
  Then mine apparell shall display before yee
  That I am Cloathd in Holy robes for glory.

The Ebb and Flow

EDWARD TAYLOR

When first thou on me Lord wrought'st thy Sweet Print,
 My heart was made thy tinder box.
 My 'ffections were thy tinder in't.
  Where fell thy Sparkes by drops.
Those holy Sparks of Heavenly Fire that came
Did ever catch and often out would flame.

But now my Heart is made thy Censar trim,
 Full of thy golden Altars fire,
 To offer up Sweet Incense in
  Unto thyselfe intire:
I finde my tinder scarce thy sparks can feel
That drop out from thy Holy flint and Steel.

Hence doubts out bud for feare thy fire in mee
 'S a mocking Ignis Fatuus
 Or lest thine Altars fire out bee,
  Its hid in ashes thus.
Yet when the bellows of thy Spirit blow
Away mine ashes, then thy fire doth glow.

LINE 14: *Ignis fatuus* is a phosphorescent light that appears to recede and then reappear. The term is used to refer to any deceptive illumination. The popular expression is *will-o'-the wisp*.

The Universal Prayer

ALEXANDER POPE

Father of all! in every age,
    In every clime adored,
By saint, by savage, and by sage,
    Jehovah, Jove, or Lord!

Thou great First Cause, least understood:
    Who all my sense confined
To know but this, that Thou art good,
    And that myself am blind;

Yet gave me, in this dark estate,
    To see the good from ill;
And binding nature fast in fate,
    Left free the human will.

What conscience dictates to be done,
    Or warns me not to do,
This, teach me more than hell to shun,
    That, more than heaven pursue.

What blessings thy free bounty gives
    Let me not cast away;
For God is paid when man receives,
    To enjoy is to obey.

Yet not to earth's contracted span
    Thy goodness let me bound,
Or think thee Lord alone of man,
    When thousand worlds are round:

Let not this weak, unknowing hand
    Presume thy bolts to throw,

And deal damnation round the land
    On each I judge thy foe.

If I am right, thy grace impart,
    Still in the right to stay;
If I am wrong oh teach my heart
    To find that better way!

Save me alike from foolish pride,
    Or impious discontent,
At aught thy wisdom has denied
    Or aught thy goodness lent.

Teach me to feel another's woe,
    To hide the fault I see;
That mercy I to others show,
    That mercy show to me.

Mean though I am, not wholly so,
    Since quickened by thy breath;
O, lead me whereso'er I go,
    Through this day's life or death!

This day, be bread and peace my lot;
    All else beneath the sun,
Thou know'st if best bestowed or not;
    and let Thy will be done.

To thee, whose temple is all space,
    Whose altar, earth, sea, skies,
One chorus let all being raise,
    All nature's incense rise!

PROBABLY WRITTEN to assert publicly Pope's orthodoxy, this poem may have been composed early in the poet's career. Pope remained Roman Catholic within a culture that despised his religion. His poetry, however, does not reflect any sentiments unique or specific to Catholicism.

Line 4: *Jehovah*, commonly used for *God* in some religious circles, is derived from the Hebrew tetragrammaton *YHWH*—a name too sacred to be spoken. In the Masoretic texts of the Hebrew Bible, the vowel signals over *YHWH* were those of *Adonai*, usually translated *Lord*. This cued readers when they encountered the name of God in writing to say *Lord* instead. Read literally, however, *YHWH* with the vowel signals of *Adonai* generates a word that medieval scholars read as *Jehovah*. This name appears several times in the King James Version of the Bible.

Jove is the more ancient and poetic name for Jupiter, the chief god of the Romans. The name *Jupiter* is thought to be an elided form of *Jove-pater*—i.e., Jove-father—or, since Jove was identified with the Greek god Zeus, *Zeus-father*.

Line 5: Aristotle (in *Metaphysics*) and later philosophers described God as the "First Cause"—that is, the "Uncaused Cause" of all that is, or the unmoved First Mover.

Our God, Our Help in Ages Past

ISAAC WATTS

Our God, our help in ages past,
   Our hope for years to come,
Our shelter from the stormy blast,
   And our eternal home.

Under the shadow of thy throne
   Thy saints have dwelt secure;
Sufficient is thine arm alone,
   And our defence is sure.

Before the hills in order stood,
   Or earth received her frame,
From everlasting thou art God,
   To endless years the same.

Thy Word commands our flesh to dust,
   'Return, ye sons of men':
All nations rose from earth at first,
   And turn to earth again.

A thousand ages in thy sight
   Are like an evening gone;
Short as the watch that ends the night
   Before the rising sun.

The busy tribes of flesh and blood
   With all their lives and cares
Are carried downwards by thy flood
   And lost in following years.

Time like an ever-rolling stream
   Bears all its sons away;

They fly forgotten as a dream
  Dies at the opening day.

Like flowery fields the nations stand
  Pleased with the morning light;
The flowers beneath the mower's hand
  Lie withering ere 'tis night.

Our God, our help in ages past,
  Our hope for years to come,
Be thou our guard while troubles last,
  And our eternal home.

AFTER THE Protestant Reformation, the churches in the Calvinist tra-
dition, suspicious of tampering with the inspired text, were initially
opposed to hymns that reworded the Psalms. The Church of England
had no such theological objections, but neither did it have any com-
posers or poets capable of transposing biblical language into hymns.
Isaac Watts, a Dissenter, was convinced that if we pray in our own lan-
guage we can certainly sing in our own language. Based on Psalm 90,
this hymn was first published in 1707 in *Hymns and Spiritual Songs* and
remains one of Watts's most popular compositions.

JAMES THOMSON

These, as they change, Almighty Father! these
Are but the varied God. The rolling year
Is full of Thee. Forth in the pleasing Spring
Thy beauty walks, Thy tenderness and love.
Wide flush the fields; the softening air is balm;
Echo the mountains round; the forest smiles;
And every sense, and every heart, is joy.
Then comes thy glory in the Summer-months,
With light and heart refulgent. Then thy sun
Shoots full perfection through the swelling year:
And oft Thy voice in dreadful thunder speaks,
And oft, at dawn, deep noon, or falling eve,
By brooks and groves, in hollow-whispering gales.
Thy bounty shines in Autumn unconfined,
And spreads a common feast for all that lives.
In Winter awful Thou! with clouds and storms
Around Thee thrown, tempest o'er tempest rolled,
Majestic darkness! On the whirlwind's wing
Riding sublime, thou bidst the world adore,
And humblest nature with Thy northern blast.

. . . .

Should fate command me to the farthest verge
Of the green earth, to distant barbarous climes,
Rivers unknown to song, where first the sun
Gilds Indian mountains, or his setting beam
Flames on the Atlantic isles, 'tis nought to me;
Since God is ever present, ever felt,
In the void waste as in the city full,
And where He vital spreads there must be joy.

When even at last the solemn hour shall come,
And wing my mystic flight to future worlds,
I cheerful will obey; there, with new powers,
Will rising wonders sing: I cannot go
Where Universal Love not smiles around,
Sustaining all yon orbs and all their sons;
From seeming evil still educing good,
And better thence again, and better still,
In infinite progression. But I lose
Myself in Him, in light ineffable!
Come then, expressive Silence, muse His praise.

THE HYMN from which this excerpt is taken concludes Thomson's
long series of poems called *The Seasons*, published in 1744. The poet's
detailed descriptions of nature were influenced by his reading of
Shaftesbury and his enthusiasm for contemporary philosophical man-
uals that put science at the service of religion. Thomson imagined a
universe created, governed by, and mysteriously united with a benev-
olent deity.

FROM *Thoughts on the Works of Providence*

PHILLIS WHEATLEY

Arise, my soul, on wings enraptur'd, rise
To praise the monarch of the earth and skies,
Whose goodness and beneficence appear,
As round its centre moves the rolling year.
. . . .

   Ador'd forever be the God unseen,
Which round the sun revolves this vast machine,
Though to his eye its mass a point appears:
Ador'd the God that whirls surrounding spheres,
Which first ordain'd that mighty Sol should reign
The peerless monarch of th'ethereal train:
Of miles twice forty millions is his height,
And yet his radiance dazzles mortal sight
So far beneath—from him th'extended earth
Vigour derives, and ev'ry flow'ry birth:

   Almighty, in these wond'rous works of thine,
What *Pow'r*, what *Wisdom*, and what *Goodness* shine?
And are thy wonders, Lord, by men explor'd,
And yet creating glory unador'd!
. . . .

   Infinite Love where'er we turn our eyes
Appears: this ev'ry creature's wants supplies;
This most is heard in Nature's constant voice,
This makes the morn, and this the eve rejoice;
This bids the fost'ring rains and dews descend
To nourish all, to serve one gen'ral end,
The good of man: yet man ungrateful pays
But little homage, and but little praise.
To him, whose works arry'd with mercy shine,
What songs should rise, how constant, how divine!

Abide with Me

Henry F. Lyte

Abide with me: fast falls the eventide;
The darkness deepens; Lord, with me abide:
When other helpers fail, and comforts flee,
Help of the helpless, O abide with me.

Swift to its close ebbs out life's little day;
Earth's joys grow dim, its glories pass away,
Change and decay in all around I see;
O thou who changest not, abide with me.

I need thy presence every passing hour;
What but thy grace can foil the tempter's power?
Who, like thyself, my guide and stay can be?
Through cloud and sunshine, Lord, abide with me.

I fear no foe, with thee at hand to bless:
Ills have no weight, and tears no bitterness.
Where is death's sting? where, grave, thy victory?
I triumph still, if thou abide with me.

Hold thou thy cross before my closing eyes;
Shine through the gloom, and point me to the skies;
Heaven's morning breaks, and earth's vain shadows flee;
In life, in death, O Lord, abide with me.

LINE 14: Cf. 1 Corinthians 15:55: "Where, O death, is your victory?
Where, O death, is your sting?"

Grace

RALPH WALDO EMERSON

How much, Preventing God! how much I owe
To the defences thou has round me set:
Example, custom, fear, occasion slow—
These scorned bondmen were my parapet.
I dare not peep over this parapet
To gauge with glance the roaring gulf below,
The depths of sin to which I had descended,
Had not these me against myself defended.

Nearer My God to Thee

SARAH FLOWER ADAMS

Nearer, my God, to Thee,
Nearer to Thee!
E'en though it be a cross
That raiseth me;
Still all my song shall be,
Nearer, my God, to Thee,
Nearer to Thee!

Though like the wanderer,
The sun gone down,
Darkness be over me,
My rest a stone;
Yet in my dreams I'd be
Nearer, my God, to Thee,
Nearer to Thee!

There let the way appear
Steps unto Heaven,
All that Thou send'st me
In mercy given;
Angels to beckon me
Nearer, my God to Thee,
Nearer to Thee!

Then, with my waking thoughts
Bright with Thy praise,
Out of my stony griefs,
Bethel I'll raise;
So by my woes to be
Nearer, my God, to Thee
Nearer to Thee!

Or, if on joyful wing,
Cleaving the sky,
Sun, moon and stars forgot,
Upward I fly,
Still all my song shall be,
Nearer, my God, to Thee,
Nearer to Thee!

THE LAST four stanzas allude to Genesis 28:10–22, the narrative describing Jacob's overnight stay in Bethel, when he slept with a stone for a pillow and dreamed of a ladder going from heaven to earth with angels ascending and descending upon it.

The Pillar of the Cloud

JOHN HENRY NEWMAN

Lead, Kindly Light, amid the encircling gloom,
  Lead Thou me on!
The night is dark, and I am far from home—
  Lead Thou me on!
Keep Thou my feet: I do not ask to see
The distant scene,—one step enough for me.

I was not ever thus, nor pray'd that Thou
  Shouldst lead me on.
I loved to choose and see my path; but now
  Lead Thou me on!
I loved the garish day, and, spite of fears,
Pride ruled my will; remember not past years.

So long Thy power hath blest me, sure it still
  Will lead me on,
O'er moor and fen, o'er crag and torrent, till
  The night is gone;
And with the morn those angel faces smile
Which I have loved long since, and lost awhile.

AT SEA, 16 JUNE 1833

THE TITLE alludes to Exodus 13:21: "The Lord went in front of them in a pillar of cloud by day, to lead them along the way."

Newman wrote this poem during a long vacation voyage that proved to be a turbulent experience. After an illness in Sicily, he boarded a boat for Marseille. When the boat was becalmed off Sardinia, Newman wrote this poem, usually designated by its opening words. He considered the whole experience a spiritual crisis and returned to England in the belief that God had given him a work to do.

ALFRED, LORD TENNYSON

Hallowed be Thy name—Halleluiah!—
Infinite Ideality!
Immeasurable Reality!
Infinite Personality!
Hallowed be Thy name—Halleluiah!

We feel we are nothing—for all is Thou and in Thee;
We feel we are something—*that* also has come from Thee;
We know we are nothing—but Thou wilt help us to be.
Hallowed be Thy name—Halleluiah!

LINE 1 is from the Lord's Prayer (Matthew 6:9 and Luke 11:2).

Halleluiah (also *[H]allelujah*) is Hebrew for "Let us praise the Lord [*jah*]." It is used twenty-three times in the Psalms, most often as an introduction or conclusion. See especially Psalms 104–150. Probably originally an exhortation to the community to pray together, it is common in Christian liturgy.

JONES VERY

I thank thee, Father, that the night is near
When I this conscious being may resign;
Whose only task Thy words of love to hear,
    And in Thy acts to find each act of mine;
A task too great to give a child like me,
The myriad-handed labors of the day
Too many for my closing eyes to see,
    Thy words too frequent for my tongue to say;
Yet when Thou see'st me burthened by Thy love
Each other gift more lovely then appears,
For dark-robed night comes hovering from above
    And all Thine other gifts to me endears;
    And while within her darkened couch I sleep,
Thine eyes untired above will constant vigils keep.

The Rock

JONES VERY

Thou art; there is no stay but in Thy love;
Thy strength remains; it built the eternal hills;
It speaks the word forever heard above,
And all creation with its presence fills;
Upon it let me stand and I shall live;
Thy strength shall fasten me forever fixed,
And to my soul its sure foundations give,
When earth and sky thy word in one has mixed;
Rooted in Thee no storm my branch shall tear;
But with each day new sap shall upward flow,
And for thy vine the clustering fruit shall bear;
That with each rain the lengthening shoots may grow,
Till o'er Thy Rock its leaves spread far and wide,
And in its green embrace its Parent hide.

God Not Afar Off

JONES VERY

Father! Thy wonders do not singly stand,
Nor far removed where feet have seldom strayed;
Around us ever lies the enchanted land,
In marvels rich to Thine own sons displayed.

In finding Thee are all things round us found!
In losing Thee are all things lost beside!
Ears have we, but in vain sweet voices sound,
And to our eyes the vision is denied.

Open our eyes that we that world may see!
Open our ears that we Thy voice may hear!
And in that spirit-land may ever be,
And feel Thy presence with us always near;

No more to wander 'mid the things of time,
No more to suffer death or earthly change;
But with the Christian's joy and faith sublime,
Through all Thy vast, eternal scenes to range.

"Heavenly Father," take to thee (102)

EMILY DICKINSON

"Heavenly Father," take to thee
The supreme iniquity,
Fashioned by thy candid hand
In a moment contraband.
Though to trust us seem to us
More respectful—"we are dust."
We apologize to Thee
For Thine own Duplicity.

The Look of Thee, what is it like? (91)

EMILY DICKINSON

The Look of Thee, what is it like?
Hast thou a hand or foot,
Or mansion of Identity,
And what is thy Pursuit?

Thy fellows,—are they Realms or Themes?
Hast thou Delight or Fear
Or longing,—and is that for us
Or values more severe?

Let change transfuse all other traits,
Enact all other blame,
But deign this least certificate—
That thou shalt be the same.

Before the Beginning

CHRISTINA GEORGINA ROSSETTI

Before the beginning Thou hast foreknown the end,
   Before the birthday the death-bed was seen of Thee:
Cleanse what I cannot cleanse, mend what I cannot mend.
   O Lord All-Merciful, be merciful to me.

While the end is drawing near I know not mine end;
   Birth I recall not, my death I cannot foresee:
O God, arise to defend, arise to befriend,
   O Lord All-Merciful, be merciful to me.

CHRISTINA GEORGINA ROSSETTI

None other Lamb, none other Name,
  None other Hope in heaven or earth or sea,
None other Hiding-place from guilt and shame,
  None beside Thee.

My faith burns low, my hope burns low,
  Only my heart's desire cries out in me
By the deep thunder of its want and woe,
  Cries out to Thee.

Lord, Thou art Life tho' I be dead,
  Love's Fire Thou art, however cold I be:
Nor heaven have I, nor place to lay my head,
  Nor home, but Thee.

The Bedridden Peasant
To an Unknowing God

THOMAS HARDY

Much wonder I—here long low-laid—
   That this dead wall should be
Betwixt the Maker and the made,
   Between Thyself and me!

For, say one puts a child to nurse,
   He eyes it now and then
To know if better it is, or worse,
   And if it mourn, and when.

But Thou, Lord, giv'st us men our day
   in helpless bondage thus
To Time and Chance, and seem'st straightway
   To think no more of us!

That some disaster cleft Thy scheme
   And tore us wide apart,
So that no cry can cross, I deem;
   For Thou art mild of heart,

And wouldst not shape and shut us in
   Where voice can not be heard:
Plainly Thou meant'st that we should win
   Thy succour by a word.

Might but Thy sense flash down the skies
   Like man's from clime to clime,
Thou wouldst not let me agonize
   Through my remaining time;

But, seeing how much Thy creatures bear—
   Lame, starved, or maimed, or blind—
Wouldst heal the ills with quickest care
   Of me and all my kind.

Then, since Thou mak'st not these things be,
   But these things dost not know,
I'll praise Thee as were shown to me
   The mercies Thou wouldst show!

"The Bedridden Peasant" was first published in 1901 in a collection called *Mr. Thomas Hardy's New Poems*, under the title "A Peasant's Philosophy." Thomas Hardy revised constantly and continued revising even previously published poems until his death in 1928. Most of the variants in manuscript differ little from the first printed editions. One manuscript suggests for part of the title: "To an Unknown God."

Ἀγνώστωι θεῶι [AGNOSTO THEO]

THOMAS HARDY

Long have I framed weak phantasies of Thee,
  O Willer masked and dumb!
  Who makest Life become,—
As though by laboring all-unknowingly,
  Like one whom reveries numb.

How much of consciousness informs Thy will,
  Thy biddings as if blind,
  Of death-inducing kind,
Nought shows to us ephemeral ones who fill
  But moments in Thy mind.

Perhaps Thy ancient rote-restricted ways
  Thy ripening rule transcends;
  That listless effort tends
To grow percipient with advance of days,
  And with percipience mends.

For, in unwonted purlieus, far and nigh,
  At whiles or short or long,
  May be discerned a wrong
Dying as of self-slaughter; whereat I
  Would raise my voice in song.

THE TITLE is taken from the Acts of the Apostles 17:23. Paul, preparing to preach to the Athenians, discovers an altar with the inscription "To an unknown god" and uses the incident as the introduction to his sermon.

Line 2: Hardy often spoke of an unconscious "Will" in the Universe that gradually achieves consciousness. Drawn to speculation about causality and necessity, he was reluctant to assert God's power over nature.

Thou Art Indeed Just, Lord

GERARD MANLEY HOPKINS

*Justus quidem tu es, Domine, si disputem tecum; verumtamen
justa loquar ad te: Quare via impiorum prosperatur? etc.*

Thou art indeed just, Lord, if I contend
With thee; but, sir, so what I plead is just.
Why do sinners' ways prosper? and why must
Disappointment all I endeavour end?

Wert thou my enemy, O thou my friend,
How wouldst thou worse, I wonder, than thou dost
Defeat, thwart me? Oh, the sots and thralls of lust
Do in spare hours more thrive than I that spend,

Sir, life upon thy cause. See, banks and brakes
Now, leavèd how thick! lacèd they are again
With fretty chervil, look, and fresh wind shakes

Them; birds build—but not I build; no, but strain,
Time's eunuch, and not breed one work that wakes.
Mine, O thou lord of life, send my roots rain.

THIS POEM was written during the last year of Hopkins's life.
    The epigraph, in the Latin Vulgate translation, is from Jeremiah 12:1:

> You will be in the right, O Lord, when I lay charges against you;
>   but let me put my case to you.
> Why does the way of the guilty prosper?
> Why do all who are treacherous thrive?

Recessional

RUDYARD KIPLING

God of our fathers, known of old,
  Lord of our far-flung battle-line,
Beneath whose awful Hand we hold
  Dominion over palm and pine—
Lord God of Hosts, be with us yet,
Lest we forget—lest we forget!

The tumult and the shouting dies;
  The Captains and the Kings depart:
Still stands Thine ancient sacrifice,
  An humble and a contrite heart.
Lord God of Hosts, be with us yet,
Lest we forget—lest we forget!

Far-called, our navies melt away;
  On dune and headland sinks the fire:
Lo, all our pomp of yesterday
  Is one with Nineveh and Tyre!
Judge of the Nations, spare us yet,
Lest we forget—lest we forget!

If, drunk with sight of power, we loose
  Wild tongues that have not Thee in awe,
Such boastings as the Gentiles use,
  Or lesser breeds without the Law—
Lord God of Hosts, be with us yet,
Lest we forget—lest we forget!

For heathen heart that puts her trust
  In reeking tube and iron shard,

All valiant dust that builds on dust,
    And guarding, calls not Thee to guard,
For frantic boast and foolish word—
Thy Mercy on Thy People, Lord!

LINES 9–10 are drawn from Psalm 51:17: "The sacrifice acceptable to God is a broken spirit; a broken and contrite heart, O God, you will not despise."

"Recessional," composed in 1897 against the backdrop of imperial England, exemplifies the cadences and pomp that attracted British readers for a generation. Kipling's biblical allusions are primarily from Hebrew Scripture. Nineveh (in ancient Assyria) and Tyre (in ancient Phoenicia) were famous for their wealth. "Lord of Hosts" is commonly used in prophetic writing and in the Psalms to describe God as sovereign. Psalm 12:3–4 condemns boasting. Psalm 20:7 alludes to those who wrongfully "take pride in their chariots."

Stand by Me

CHARLES A. TINDLEY

When the storms of life are raging,
Stand by me, stand by me.
When the storms of life are raging,
Stand by me, stand by me.

When the world is tossing me,
Like a ship out on the sea:
Thou who knowest all about it,
Stand by your child, stand by me.

In the midst of persecution,
Stand by me, stand by me.
In the midst of persecution,
Stand by me, stand by me.

When my foes in battle array
Undertake to stop my way,
Thou who rescued Paul and Silas,
Stand by me, stand by me.

When I'm growing old and feeble,
Stand by me, stand by me.
When I'm growing old and feeble,
Stand by me, stand by me.

When my life becomes a burden,
And I'm nearing chilly Jordan
O thou Lily of the Valley,
Stand by me, stand by me.

LINE 15: Silas, also known as Silvanus, was a companion to Paul and accompanied him on several of his missionary journeys. See, for example, 2 Thessalonians 1:1.

Within the African-American musical tradition, gospel songs are sometimes distinguished from spirituals. Gospel music emerged in the 1930s as part of the jazz tradition, and these songs were made popular by preachers who sang and performed, usually in the Holiness churches. Tindley's hymns often combined blues melodies and tones with conventional and revivalist religious hymnody.

The version of "Stand By Me" sung by Ben E. King in the 1960s became a hit record and later, in the 1980s, served as the title song for the movie *Stand by Me*.

The Hands of God

D. H. LAWRENCE

It is a fearful thing to fall into the hands of the living God.
But it is a much more fearful thing to fall out of them.

Did Lucifer fall through knowledge?
oh then, pity him, pity him that plunge!

Save me, O God, from falling into the ungodly knowledge
of myself as I am without God.
Let me never know, O God
let me never know what I am or should be
when I have fallen out of your hands, the hands of the
    living God.

That awful and sickening endless sinking, sinking
through the slow, corruptive levels of disintegrative
    knowledge
when the self has fallen from the hands of God,
and sinks, seething and sinking, corrupt
and sinking still, in depth after depth of disintegrative
    consciousness
sinking in the endless undoing, the awful katabolism into
    the abyss!
even of the soul, fallen from the hands of God!

Save me from that, O God!
Let me never know myself apart from the living God!

LINE 1: "It is a fearful thing" is from Hebrews 10:31.

LINE 3: "Did Lucifer fall . . . ?": "Lucifer" is a translation of the He-
brew for "Day Star" in Isaiah 14:12. "How you are fallen from heaven,

O Day Star, son of Dawn!" The passage, referring to the fall of the King of Babylon, was later associated with Luke 10:18, where Jesus says, "I watched Satan fall from heaven like a flash of lightning." The popular tradition that makes Lucifer (Satan) the leader of the angels who was driven from heaven when he rebelled against God is not in the Bible. It was made poetically immortal, however, in Milton's *Paradise Lost*.

FROM *Eleven Addresses to the Lord* — (1)

JOHN BERRYMAN

Master of beauty, craftsman of the snowflake,
inimitable contriver,
endower of Earth so gorgeous & different from the
    boring Moon.
thank you for such as it is my gift.

I have made up a morning prayer to you
containing with precision everything that most matters.
'According to Thy will' the thing begins.
It took me off & on two days. It does not aim at eloquence.

You have come to my rescue again & again
in my impassable, sometimes despairing years.
You have allowed my brilliant friends to destroy themselves
and I am still here, severely damaged, but functioning.

Unknowable, as I am unknown to my guinea pigs:
how can I 'love' you?
I only as far as gratitude & awe
confidently and absolutely go.

I have no idea whether we live again.
It doesn't seem likely
from either the scientific or the philosophical point of view
but certainly all things are possible to you,

and I believe as fixedly in the Resurrection-appearances to
    Peter and to Paul

  as I believe I sit in this blue chair.
Only that may have been a special case
to establish their initiatory faith.

Whatever your end may be, accept my amazement.
May I stand until death forever at attention
for any your least instruction or enlightenment.
I even feel sure you will assist me again, Master of insight
    & beauty.

THIS IS the first of a sequence of eleven poems published as part four of *Love and Fame* (1971). The title of the collection suggests Keats's "When I Have Fears," which ends with "Till Love and Fame to nothingness do sink." The collection, written shortly before Berryman's suicide, is intensely self-revelatory.

And What Do I Owe You, God

JACK KEROUAC

And what do I owe You, God, for my gifts:
I owe you perspiration and suffering and
all the dark night of my life:
God I owe you godliness and diligence,
God I owe you this blackest loneliness,
and terrified dreams—
but humbleness, God, I have none and
I owe it You: for I would have You
reach down a hand to me, to help me
up to You—Oh I am not humble.
Give me this last gift, God, and I *will*
be humble, I *will* owe You humbleness,
but only give me the gift.
Spit in my soul, God, for asking and
always asking, and for not giving and
owing what I have given, and give,
and shall give: God make me *give*.
Old Job there of the three thousand five
hundred years a-mouldering in his grave,
Old Job there is your servant, God:
forgive me for my youth, then forgive
me for *it*, God, oh make me a giver.

LINE 18: "Old Job" refers to the title character of the biblical Book of
Job, whose personal suffering drove him to question God's justice and
finally to submit to the mystery of God's power and wisdom.

This untitled poem is one of many prayers, hymns, and intensely
personal essays found in Jack Kerouac's unpublished writings.

TRINIDAD TARROSA SUBIDO

God, but I do
Worship you.
Nun-like adoration? No.
Like a bird? So:

faith
natural as breath.

I shall pray when prayer is
lip's caprice
like the thrilling of a bird
impulse-stirred.

God to me, and prayer
is as song to bird, and air:
elemental,
not sacramental.

Matins

LOUISE GLÜCK

Unreachable father, when we were first
exiled from heaven, you made
a replica, a place in one sense
different from heaven, being
designed to teach a lesson: otherwise
the same—beauty on either side, beauty
without alternative— Except
we didn't know what was the lesson. Left alone,
we exhausted each other. Years
of darkness followed; we took turns
working the garden, the first tears
filling our eyes as earth
misted with petals, some
dark red, some flesh colored—
We never thought of you
whom we were learning to worship.
We merely knew it wasn't human nature to love
only what returns love.

THIS IS one of seven poems entitled "Matins" in Glück's collection
The Wild Iris (1992). Matins is traditionally the first prayer of the morn-
ing in monastic tradition, sung anytime from just after midnight to be-
fore dawn.

PART THREE

About God: The Poem

The Lord is my shepherd, I shall not want.
    He makes me lie down in green pastures;
he leads me beside still waters;
    he restores my soul.
He leads me in right paths
    for his name's sake.
Even though I walk through the darkest valley,
    I fear no evil;
for you are with me;
    your rod and your staff—
they comfort me.
You prepare a table before me
    in the presence of my enemies;
you anoint my head with oil;
    my cup overflows.
Surely goodness and mercy shall follow me
    all the days of my life,
and I shall dwell in the house of the Lord
    my whole life long.

LINE 10: "the darkest valley" can also be translated as "the valley of death."

Throughout both Hebrew Scripture and the New Testament, the shepherd is a common image for a king or leader. See, for example, Jeremiah 23:1: "Woe to the shepherds who destroy and scatter the sheep of my pasture! says the Lord." Ezekiel 34:6 extends the image: "my sheep were scattered over all the face of the earth, with no one to search or seek for them." In John 10:11, Jesus says, "I am the good shepherd."

FROM *Hymn of Heavenly Beauty*

EDMUND SPENSER

Cease then my tongue, and lend unto my mind
Leave to bethink how great that beauty is
Whose utmost parts so beautiful I find—
How much more those essential parts of his,
His truth, his love, his wisdom and his bliss,
His grace, his doom, his mercy, and his might,
By which he lends us of himself a sight!

Those unto all he daily doth display,
And show himself in th' image of his grace
As in a looking glass, through which he may
Be seen of all his creatures vile and base,
That are unable else to see his face—
His glorious face, which glistereth else so bright
That th'angels selves cannot endure his sight.

But we frail wights, whose sight cannot sustain
The sun's bright beams when he on us doth shine
But that their points, rebutted back again,
Are dulled—how can we see with feeble eyne
The glory of that majesty divine,
In sight of whom both sun and moon are dark
Comparèd to his least resplendent spark?

The means, therefore, which unto us is lent
Him to behold, is on his works to look,
Which he hath made in beauty excellent,
And in the same as in a brazen book,
To read enregistered in every nook

His goodness, which his beauty doth declare;
For all that's good is beautiful and fair.

—LL. 106–126

EDMUND SPENSER wrote four long poems (*Fowre Hymnes*), two about earthly love and beauty and two about heavenly love and beauty. "An Hymne of Heavenly Beautie," from which this selection is taken, is about God. The others are about Cupid, Venus, and Christ. All of them blend Puritanism, especially the writings of John Calvin, and neoplatonism. God's beauty is reflected in material creation.

Line 115: "as in a looking glass": Cf. 1 Corinthians 13:12: "For now we see in a mirror, dimly, but then we will see face to face."

To Find God

ROBERT HERRICK

Weigh me the fire; or canst thou find
A way to measure out the wind?
Distinguish all those floods that are
Mixed in that wat'ry theater,
And taste thou them as saltless there,
As in their channel first they were.
Tell me the people that do keep
Within the kingdoms of the deep;
Or, fetch me back that cloud again,
Beshivered into seeds of rain.
Tell me the motes, dust, sands, and spears
Of corn, when summer shakes his ears.
Show me that world of stars, and whence
They noiseless spill their influence:
This if thou canst, then show me Him
That rides the glorious cherubim.

THE SENTIMENTS of Herrick in this poem echo the long reply of
God to Job in chapters 38–41 of the Book of Job, especially the dis-
course beginning at 40:7, "I will question you, and you declare to me."

Line 16: "cherubim" in this poem refers to the second of the tradi-
tional nine choirs or levels of angels, the highest being the seraphim.

God's Anger without Affection

ROBERT HERRICK

GOD when He's angry here with any one,
His wrath is free from perturbation;
And when we think His looks are sowre and grim,
The alteration is in us, not Him.

Love (3)

GEORGE HERBERT

Love bade me welcome: yet my soul drew back,
    Guilty of dust and sin.
But quick-eyed Love, observing me grow slack
    From my first entrance in,
Drew nearer to me, sweetly questioning,
    If I lacked anything.

"A guest," I answered, "worthy to be here":
    Love said, "You shall be he."
"I, the unkind, ungrateful? Ah, my dear,
    I cannot look on thee."
Love took my hand, and smiling did reply,
    "Who made the eyes but I?"

"Truth, Lord, but I have marred them: let my shame
    Go where it doth deserve."
"And know you not," says Love, "who bore the blame?"
    "My dear, then I will serve."
"You must sit down," says Love, "and taste my meat."
    So I did sit and eat.

The Collar

GEORGE HERBERT

I struck the board, and cried, "No more!
          I will abroad.
What? shall I ever sigh and pine?
My lines and life are free; free as the road,
     Loose as the wind, as large as store.
          Shall I be still in suit?
     Have I no harvest but a thorn
     To let me blood, and not restore
What I have lost with cordial fruit?
               Sure there was wine
Before my sighs did dry it: there was corn
          Before my tears did drown it.
     Is the year only lost to me?
          Have I no bays to crown it?
No flowers, no garlands gay? All blasted?
          All wasted?
     Not so, my heart: but there is fruit,
          And thou hast hands.
     Recover all thy sigh-blown age
On double pleasures: leave thy cold dispute
Of what is fit, and not. Forsake thy cage,
          Thy rope of sands,
Which petty thoughts have made, and made to thee
     Good cable, to enforce and draw,
          And be thy law,
While thou didst wink and wouldst not see.
          Away; take heed:
          I will abroad.

Call in thy death's head there; tie up thy fears.

           He that forbears

     To suit and serve his need,

           Deserves his load."

But as I raved and grew more fierce and wild

           At every word,

Methought I heard one calling, "*Child*!"

           And I replied, "*My Lord*."

The Revival

HENRY VAUGHAN

Unfold, unfold! take in his light,
Who makes thy cares more short than night.
The joys, which with his day-star rise,
He deals to all but drowsy eyes:
And what the men of this world miss,
Some drops and dews of future bliss.
   Hark how his winds have changed their note,
   nd with warm whispers call thee out.
The frosts are past, the storms are gone,
And backward life at last comes on.
The lofty groves in express joys
Reply unto the turtle's voice,
And here in dust and dirt, O here
The lilies of his love appear!

THE SONNET is an echo of the Song of Solomon (2:11–12):

> For now the winter is past,
>   the rain is over and gone.
> The flowers appear on the earth;
>   the time of singing has come,
> and the voice of the turtledove
>   is heard in our land.

JOHN MILTON

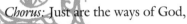

Chorus: Just are the ways of God,
And justifiable to Men;
Unless there be who think not God at all:
If any be, they walk obscure;
For of such Doctrine never was there School,
But the heart of the Fool,
And no man therein Doctor but himself.

—LL. 293–299

IN THIS first section of *Samson Agonistes*, based on the biblical story of Samson in the Book of Judges 13–16, Samson and the chorus of Hebrews contrast the historical victories of the past with present disaster. The defense of God's ways can be compared to Revelation 15:3: "Just and true are your ways, King of the nations."

Line 298: Milton alludes here to Psalm 14:1: "Fools say in their hearts, 'There is no God.'"

from Book 2

But now I feel I hunger, which declares
Nature hath need of what she asks; yet God
Can satisfy that need some other way,
Though hunger still remain: so it remain
Without this body's wasting, I content me,
And from the sting of Famine fear no harm,
Nor mind it fed with better thoughts that feed,
Mee hung'ring more to do my Father's will.

—LL. 252–259

PARADISE REGAINED is Milton's account of the three temptations of Christ recorded in Luke 4:1–12. In the gospel account, Satan first suggests to Jesus that he turn stone to bread, then that he accept all the kingdoms of the world as a gift from Satan, and finally that he throw himself from the pinnacle of the Temple to demonstrate God's protection. Milton includes the temptation to transform stone to bread in Book I of *Paradise Regained*. Jesus rejects the offer peremptorily. Book II, from which this passage is taken, describes Satan's plan to approach Christ again, this time with the vision of a Roman banquet. The night before the vision, Jesus, who has been fasting for forty days and nights, prays.

Line 259: See John 4:34: "My food is to do the will of him who sent me."

ALEXANDER POPE

8. See, through this air, this ocean, and this earth,
All matter quick, and bursting into birth.
Above, how high, progressive life may go!
Around, how wide!, how deep extend below!
Vast chain of being! Which from God began,
Natures ethereal, human, angel, man,
Beast, bird, fish, insect, what no eye can see,
No glass can reach; from infinite to thee,
From thee to nothing.—On superior powers
Were we to press, inferior might on ours:
Or in the full creation leave a void,
Where, one step broken, the great scale's destroyed:
From nature's chain whatever link you strike,
Tenth or ten thousandth, breaks the chain alike.
    And, if each system in gradation roll
Alike essential to the amazing whole,
The least confusion but in one, not all
That system only, but the whole must fall.
Let earth unbalanced from her orbit fly,
Planets and suns run lawless through the sky,
Let ruling angels from their spheres be hurled,
Being on being wrecked, and world on world,
Heaven's whole foundations to their center nod,
And Nature tremble to the throne of God:
All this dread ORDER break—for whom? For thee?
Vile worm!—oh, madness, pride, impiety!
    9. What if the foot, ordained the dust to tread,
Or hand, to toil, aspired to be the head?
What if the head, the eye, or ear repined

To serve mere engines to the ruling mind?
Just as absurd for any part to claim
To be another, in this general frame:
Just as absurd, to mourn the tasks or pains,
The great directing mind of all ordains.

   All are but parts of one stupendous whole,
Whose body nature is, and God the soul;
That, changed through all, and yet in all the same,
Great in the earth, as in the ethereal frame,
Warms in the sun, refreshes in the breeze,
Glows in the stars, and blossoms in the trees,
Lives through all life, extends through all extent,
Spreads undivided, operates unspent;
Breathes in our soul, informs our mortal part,
As full, as perfect, in a hair as heart:
As full, as perfect, in vile man that mourns,
As the rapt seraph that adores and burns:
To him no high, no low, no great, no small;
He fills, he bounds, connects, and equals all.

—EPISTLE I, LL. 233–280

THE *Essay on Man* is divided into four epistles. This selection is from Epistle I, sections 8 and 9. The entire poem is not so much about man as about the whole moral universe that includes man. To Pope, the "chain of being" connects everything and justifies everything. It is static and unchangeable.

   Section 9, "What if the foot, ordained the dust to tread," suggests Paul's First Letter to the Corinthians 12:14–26 ("If the foot would say, 'Because I am not a hand, I do not belong to the body,' that would not make it any less a part of the body." Pope's theology, however, is quite different. He is not talking about the Body of Christ but the body of Nature, a world where reason can restrain self-love and the *status quo* proceeds from the divine will: "Whatever is, is right" (Epistle I, section 10, line 294).

WILLIAM COWPER

from Book 6, "The Winter Walk at Noon"

The Lord of all, himself through all diffus'd,
Sustains, and is the life of all that lives.
Nature is but a name for an effect,
Whose cause is God. He feeds the secret fire
By which the mighty process is maintained,
Who sleeps not, is not weary; in whose sight
Slow circling ages are as transient days;
Whose work is without labor; whose designs
No flaw deforms, no difficulty thwarts;
And whose beneficence no charge exhausts.
Him blind antiquity profaned, not served,
With self-taught rites, and under various names,
Female and male, Pomona, Pales, Pan,
And Flora, and Vertumnus; peopling earth
With tutelary goddesses and gods
That were not; and commending, as they would,
To each some province, garden, field, or grove.
But all are under one. One spirit—His
Who wore the platted thorns with bleeding brows—
Rules universal nature. Not a flower
But shows some touch, in freckle, streak, or stain,
Of his unrivaled pencil. He inspires
Their balmy odors, and imparts their hues,
And bathes their eyes with nectar, and includes,
In grains as countless as the sea-side sands,
The forms with which he sprinkles all the earth.

Happy who walks with him! Whom what he finds
Of flavor or of scent in fruit or flow'r,
Or what he views of beautiful or grand
In nature, from the broad majestic oak
To the green blade that twinkles in the sun,
Prompts with remembrance of a present God!

—LL. 221–252

LINE 7: Cf. 2 Peter 3:8: "with the Lord one day is like a thousand years, and a thousand years are like one day."

The Divine Image

WILLIAM BLAKE

To Mercy, Pity, Peace, and Love
All pray in their distress;
And to these virtues of delight
Return their thankfulness.

For Mercy, Pity, Peace and Love
Is God, our Father dear,
And Mercy, Pity, Peace and Love
Is man, his child and care.

For Mercy has a human heart,
Pity a human face,
And Love, the human form divine,
And Peace the human dress.

Then every man, of every clime,
That prays in his distress,
Prays to the human form divine
Love, Mercy, Pity Peace.

And all must love the human form
In heathen, Turk or Jew;
Where Mercy, Love & Pity dwell
There God is dwelling too.

MORE LUCID than Blake's long, startlingly imaginative works, such as *The Marriage of Heaven and Hell*, this poem reveals the poet's understanding of the relationship between God and human compassion. It echoes the medieval *ubi caritas* theme, "Where love is, there is God," but in Blake, God and humankind are more closely identified than in orthodox religion. Later, in *The Everlasting Gospel* (1810), he would argue that the true God is within man: "Thy own humanity learn to adore."

On Another's Sorrow

WILLIAM BLAKE

Can I see another's woe,
And not be in sorrow too?
Can I see another's grief,
And not seek for kind relief?

Can I see a falling tear,
And not feel my sorrow's share?
Can a father see his child
Weep, nor be with sorrow fill'd?

Can a mother sit and hear
An infant groan, an infant fear?
No, no! never can it be!
Never, never can it be!

And can he who smiles on all
Hear the wren with sorrows small,
Hear the small bird's grief & care,
Hear the woes that infants bear,

And not sit beside the nest,
Pouring pity in their breast;
And not sit the cradle near
Weeping tear on infant's tear:

And not sit both night & day,
Wiping all our tears away?
O no, never can it be!
Never, never can it be!

He doth give his joy to all;
He becomes an infant small;

He becomes a man of woe;
He doth feel the sorrow too.

Think not thou canst sigh a sigh,
And thy maker is not by;
Think not thou canst weep a tear,
And thy maker is not near.

O! He gives to us his joy
That our grief he may destroy;
Till our grief is fled & gone
He doth sit by us and moan.

Line 9: Cf. Isaiah 49:15: "Can a woman forget her nursing child, or show no compassion for the child of her womb? Even these may forget, yet I will not forget you."

SAMUEL TAYLOR COLERIDGE

There is one Mind, one omnipresent Mind,
Omnific. His most holy name is Love.
Truth of subliming import! With the which
Who feeds and saturates his constant soul,
He from his small particular orbit flies
With blest outstarting! From himself he flies,
Stands in the sun, and with no partial gaze
Views all creation; and he loves it all,
And blesses it, and calls it very good!
This is indeed to dwell with the Most High!
Cherubs and rapture-trembling Seraphim
Can press no nearer to the Almighty's throne.
But that we roam unconscious, or with hearts
Unfeeling of our universal Sire,
And that in His vast family no Cain
Injures uninjured (in her best-aimed blow
Victorious Murder a blind Suicide)
Haply for this some younger Angel now
Looks down on Human Nature: and, behold!
A sea of blood bestrewed with wrecks, where mad
Embattling Interests on each other rush
With unhelmed rage!

       'Tis the sublime of man,
Our noontide Majesty, to know ourselves
Parts and proportions of one wondrous whole!
This fraternizes man, this constitutes
Our charities and bearings. But 'tis God

Diffused through all, that doth make all one whole;
This the worst superstition, him except
Aught to desire, Supreme Reality!
The plenitude and permanence of bliss!

—LL. 114–143

INCLUDED IN *Poems on Various Subjects* in 1796, "Religious Musings,"
written by the young Coleridge, describes an intuitive faith shaped by
neoplatonism, quite different from the rationalism that dominated
philosophical inquiry in the eighteenth century. The poem was direct-
ed against English politics that argued for the war with France as a
Christian cause.

Line 124: Cherubs (or cherubim) and seraphim are the eighth and
ninth ranks of the traditional nine choirs of angels. They are under-
stood to be the angels closest to God.

God Scatters Beauty

WALTER SAVAGE LANDOR

God scatters beauty as he scatters flowers
O'er the wide earth, and tells us all are ours.
A hundred lights in every temple burn,
And at each shrine I bend my knee in turn.

A Child's Thought of God

Elizabeth Barrett Browning

I

They say that God lives very high;
   But if you look above the pines
You cannot see our God; and why?

II

And if you dig down in the mines
   You never see Him in the gold;
Though from Him all that's glory shines.

III

God is so good, He wears a fold
   Of heaven and earth across his face—
Like secrets kept, for love, untold.

IV

But still I feel that His embrace
   Slides down by thrills, through all things made,
Through sight and sound of every place:

V

As if my tender mother laid
   On my shut lips her kisses' pressure,
Half-waking me at night, and said
   "Who kissed you through the dark, dear guesser?"

The Higher Pantheism

ALFRED, LORD TENNYSON

The sun, the moon, the stars, the seas, the hills and the
   plains,—
Are not these, O Soul, the Vision of Him who reigns?

Is not the Vision He, tho' He be not that which
   He seems?
Dreams are true while they last, and do we not live
   in dreams?

Earth, these solid stars, this weight of body and limb,
Are they not sign and symbol of thy division from Him?

Dark is the world to thee; thyself art the reason why,
For is He not all but thou, that hast power to feel "I am I"?

Glory about thee, without thee; and thou fulfillest
   thy doom,
Making Him broken gleams and a stifled splendor and
   gloom.

Speak to Him, thou, for He hears, and Spirit with Spirit
   can meet--
Closer is He than breathing, and nearer than hands
   and feet.

God is law, say the wise; O Soul, and let us rejoice,
For if He thunder by law the thunder is yet His voice.

Law is God, say some: no God at all, says the fool;
For all we have power to see is a straight staff bent in
   a pool;

And the ear of man cannot hear, and the eye of man
    cannot see;
But if we could see and hear, this Vision—were it
    not He?

LINE 15: Cf. Psalm 14:1: "The fool says in his heart, There is no God."
    Tennyson struggled to reconcile traditional Christian piety with new theories of science and the developing methods of scriptural analysis, often called "the Higher Criticism." The title of this poem published in *The Holy Grail and Other Poems* (1869) echoes that phrase. "God and the spiritual are the only real and true," he once wrote to his son. Tennyson directs his poetic argument against pantheism, atheism, and the assertion that nature's laws are "God."

No coward soul is mine

EMILY BRONTË

No coward soul is mine
No trembler in the world's storm-troubled sphere;
I see Heaven's glories shine,
And faith shines equal, arming me from Fear

O God within my breast,
Almighty, ever-present Deity!
Life, that in me hast rest,
As I, Undying Life, have power in Thee!

Vain are the thousand creeds
That move men's hearts, unutterably vain,
Worthless as withered weeds
Or idle froth amid the boundless main

To waken doubt in one
Holding so fast by thy infinity;
So surely anchored on
The steadfast rock of Immortality.

With wide-embracing love
Thy spirit animates eternal years,
Pervades and broods above,
Changes, sustains, dissolves, creates, and rears.

Though Earth and moon were gone,
And suns and universes ceased to be,
And THOU wert left alone,
Every Existence would exist in Thee

There is not room for Death
Nor atom that his might could render void;

Since THOU art Being and Breath
And what THOU art may never be destroyed.

CHARLOTTE BRONTË has noted that these lines, dated 2 January 1846, were the last Emily Brontë ever wrote.

All circumstances are the frame (145)

EMILY DICKINSON

All circumstances are the frame
In which His Face is set,
All latitudes exist for His
Sufficient continent.
The light His Action and the dark
The Leisure of His Will,
In Him Existence serve, or set
A force illegible.

God-Forgotten

THOMAS HARDY

I towered far, and lo! I stood within
The presence of the Lord Most High,
Sent thither by the sons of Earth, to win
　　Some answer to their cry.

—"The Earth, sayest thou? The Human race?
By Me created? Sad its lot?
Nay: I have no remembrance of such place:
　　Such world I fashioned not."—

—"O Lord, forgive me when I say
Thou spakest the word that made it all."—
"The Earth of men—let me bethink me. . . . Yea!
　　I dimly do recall

"Some tiny sphere I built long back
(Mid millions of such shapes of mine)
So named . . . It perished, surely—not a wrack
　　Remaining, or a sign?

"It lost my interest from the first,
My aims therefor succeeding ill;
Haply it died of doing as it durst?"—
　　"Lord, it existeth still."—

"Dark, then, its life! For not a cry
Of aught it bears do I now hear;
Of its own act the threads were snapt whereby
　　Its plaints had reached mine ear.

"It used to ask for gifts of good,
Till came its severance self-entailed,
When sudden silence on that side ensued,
　　And has till now prevailed.

"All other orbs have kept in touch;
    Their voicings reach me speedily:
Thy people took upon them overmuch
        In sundering them from me!

"And it is strange—though sad enough—
    Earth's race should think that one whose call
Frames, daily, shining spheres of flawless stuff
        Must heed their tainted ball! . . .

"But say'st thou 'tis by pangs distraught,
    And strife, and silent suffering?—
Sore grieved am I that injury should be wrought
        Even on so poor a thing!

"Thou shouldst have learnt that *Not to Mend*
    For Me could mean but *Not to Know*:
Hence, Messengers! and straightway put an end
        To what men undergo." . . .

Homing at dawn, I thought to see
    One of the Messengers standing by.
—O childish thought! . . . Yet still it comes to me
        When trouble hovers nigh.

                                    [1902]

LINE 10: In Genesis 1, God is described as "speaking" the world into existence.

Published in 1901 in *Poems of the Past and the Present*, this dialogue between an unnamed speaker and God expresses Hardy's persistent belief, drawn from his reading of Eduard von Hartmann's *The Philosophy of the Unconscious*, that God is not aware of human suffering, that He is an unconscious world-mind. Hardy wrote a number of poems expressing the Victorian version of the "death of God," generated by new scientific and historical questioning of the historicity of the biblical texts. Hardy attended church and was deeply influenced by the Bible, but he argued for a rational Christianity, insisting that what was beyond appearances was unknowable.

Pied Beauty

GERARD MANLEY HOPKINS

Glory be to God for dappled things—
  For skies of couple-colour as a brinded cow;
    For rose-moles all in stipple upon trout that swim;
Fresh-firecoal chestnut-falls; finches' wings;
  Landscape plotted and pieced—fold, fallow, and plough;
    And áll trades, their gear and tackle and trim.

All things counter, original, spáre, strange;
  Whatever is fickle, frecklèd (who knows how?)
    With swíft, slów; sweet, sóur; adázzle, dím;
He fathers-forth whose beauty is pást change;
                    Práise hím.

COMPOSED IN 1877, the year of Hopkins's ordination to the priest-hood, "Pied Beauty" expresses a theme important to the poet's spiri-tuality: that the world and particular objects in the world are directly knowable, and that God is knowable primarily through such objects. The particularity of objects and their internal unity he described as "in-scape." He was influenced by Duns Scotus, a medieval Catholic think-er, whom Hopkins had begun reading in 1872.

The changelessness of God is expressed in James 1:17: "Every gen-erous act of giving, with every perfect gift, is from above, coming down from the Father of lights, with whom there is no variation or shadow due to change."

The Hound of Heaven

FRANCIS THOMPSON

I fled Him, down the nights and down the days;
    I fled Him, down the arches of the years;
I fled Him, down the labyrinthine ways
    Of my own mind; and in the mist of tears
I hid from Him, and under running laughter.
            Up vistaed hopes I sped;
            And shot, precipitated,
Adown Titanic glooms of chasmèd fears,
    From those strong Feet that followed, followed after.
            But with unhurrying chase,
            And unperturbèd pace,
        Deliberate speed, majestic instancy,
            They beat—and a Voice beat
            More instant than the Feet—
        "All things betray thee, who betrayest Me."

            I pleaded, outlaw-wise,
By many a hearted casement, curtained red,
    Trellised with intertwining charities;
(For, though I knew His love Who followèd,
            Yet was I sore adread
Lest, having Him, I must have naught beside);
But, if one little casement parted wide,
    The gust of His approach would clash it to:
    Fear wist not to evade, as Love wist to pursue.
Across the margent of the world I fled,
        And troubled the gold gateways of the stars,
Smiting for shelter on their clangèd bars;
            Fretted to dulcet jars

And silvern chatter the pale ports o' the moon.
I said to Dawn: Be sudden—to Eve: Be soon;
   With thy young skiey bossoms heap me over
        From this tremendous Lover—
Float thy vague veil about me, lest He see!
   I tempted all His servitors, but to find
My own betrayal in their constancy,
In faith to Him their fickleness to me,
   Their traitorous trueness, and their loyal deceit,
To all swift things for swiftness did I sue;
   Clung to the whistling mane of every wind.
        But whether they swept, smoothly fleet,
     The long savannahs of the blue;
        Or whether, Thunder-driven.
        They clanged his chariot 'thwart a heaven,
Plashy with flying lightnings round the spurn of their feet:—
   Fear wist not to evade as Love wist to pursue.
       Still with unhurrying chase,
       And unperturbèd pace,
     Deliberate speed, majestic instancy,
      Came on the following Feet,
      And a Voice above their beat—
   "Naught shelters thee, who wilt not shelter Me."

I sought no more that after which I strayed
       In face of man or maid;
But still within the little children's eyes
       Seems something, something that replies;
They at least are for me, surely for me!
I turned to them very wistfully;
But, just as their young eyes grew sudden fair
      With dawning answers there,
Their angel plucked them from me by the hair.
"Come then, ye other children, Nature's—share
With me" (said I) "your delicate fellowship;
     Let me greet you lip to lip,

Let me twine with you caresses,
　　Wantoning
With our Lady-Mother's vagrant tresses,
　　Banqueting
With her in her wind-walled palace,
Underneath her azured daïs
Quaffing, as your taintless way is,
　　From a chalice
Lucent-weeping out of the dayspring."
　　　So it was done:
I in their delicate fellowship was one—
Drew the bolt of Nature's secrecies.
　　I knew all the swift importings
　　On the wilful face of skies;
　　I knew how the clouds arise
　　Spumèd of the wild sea-snortings;
　　　All that's born or dies
　　Rose and drooped with—made them shapers
Of mine own moods, or wailful or divine—
　　With them joyed and was bereaven.
　　I was heavy with the even,
　　When she lit her glimmering tapers
　　Round the day's dead sanctities.
　　I laughed in the morning's eyes.
I triumphed and I saddened with all weather,
　　Heaven and I wept together,
And its sweet tears were salt with mortal mine;
Against the red throb of its sunset-heart
　　I laid my own to beat
　　And share commingling heat;
But not by that, by that, was eased my human smart.
In vain my tears were wet on Heaven's gray cheek.
For ah! we know not what each other says,
　　These things and I; in sound *I* speak—
Their sound is but their stir; they speak by silences.
Nature, poor stepdame, cannot slake my drouth;

Let her, if she would owe me,
Drop yon blue bosom—veil of sky, and show me
The breasts o' her tenderness:
Never did any milk of hers once bless
My thirsting mouth.
Nigh and nigh draws the chase,
With unperturbèd pace,
Deliberate speed, majestic instancy;
And past those noisèd Feet
A voice comes yet more fleet—
"Lo, naught contents thee, who content'st not Me."

Naked I wait Thy love's uplifted stroke!
My harness piece by piece Thou has hewn from me,
And smitten me to my knee;
I am defenseless utterly.
I slept, methinks, and woke,
And, slowly gazing, find me stripped in sleep.
In the rash lustihead of my young powers,
I shook the pillaring hours
And pulled my life upon me; grimed with smears,
I stand amid the dust o' the mounded years—
My mangled youth lies dead beneath the heap.
My days have crackled and gone up in smoke,
Have puffed and burst as sun-starts on a stream.
Yea, faileth now even dream
The dreamer, and the lute the lutanist;
Even the linked fantasies, in whose blossomy twist
I swung the earth a trinket at my wrist,
Are yielding; cords of all too weak account
For earth with heavy griefs so overplussed.
Ah! is Thy love indeed
A weed, albeit an amaranthine weed,
Suffering no flowers except its own to mount?
Ah! must—
Designer infinite!—

Ah! must Thou char the wood ere Thou canst limn with it?
My freshness spent its wavering shower i' the dust;
And now my heart is as a broken fount,
Wherein tear-droppings stagnate, spilt down ever
  From the dank thoughts that shiver
Upon the sighful branches of my mind.
  Such is; what is to be?
The pulp so bitter, how shall taste the rind?
I dimly guess what Time in mists confounds;
Yet ever and anon a trumpet sounds
From the hid battlements of Eternity;
Those shaken mists a space unsettle, then
Round the half-glimpsèd turrets slowly wash again.
  But not ere him who summoneth
  I first have seen, enwound
With glooming robes purpureal, cypress—crowned;
His name I know, and what his trumpet saith.
Whether man's heart or life it be which yields
  Thee harvest, must Thy harvest fields
  Be dunged with rotten death?

  Now of that long pursuit
  Comes on at hand the bruit;
  That Voice is round me like a bursting sea:
   "And is thy earth so marred,
   Shattered in shard on shard?
  Lo, all things fly thee, for thou fliest Me!
  Strange, piteous, futile thing,
Wherefore should any set thee love apart?
Seeing none but I makes much of naught"(He said),
"And human love needs human meriting:
  How has thou merited—
Of all man's clotted clay the dingiest clot?
  Alack, thou knowest not
How little worthy of any love thou art!
Whom wilt thou find to love ignoble thee

Save Me, save only Me?
All which I took from thee I did but take,
        Not for thy harms,
But just that thou might'st seek it in My arms.
        All which thy child's mistake
Fancies as lost, I have stored for thee at home:
        Rise, clasp My hand, and come!"

    Halts by me that footfall:
    Is my gloom, after all,
Shade of His Hand, outstretched caressingly?
    "Ah, fondest, blindest, weakest,
    I am He Whom thou seekest!
Thou dravest love from thee, who dravest Me."

STEPHEN CRANE

The livid lightnings flashed in the clouds;
The leaden thunders crashed.
A worshipper raised his arm.
"Hearken! Hearken! The voice of God!"

"Not so," said a man.
"The voice of God whispers in the heart
So softly
That the soul pauses,
Making no noise,
And strives for these melodies,
Distant, sighing, like faintest breath,
And all the being is still to hear."

THE POEM recalls the story of Elijah told in 1 Kings 19:11–12: "Now there was a great wind, so strong that it was splitting mountains and breaking rocks in pieces before the Lord, but the Lord was not in the wind; and after the wind an earthquake, but the Lord was not in the earthquake; and after the earthquake a fire, but the Lord was not in the fire; and after the fire a sound of sheer silence."

He's Jus' de Same Today

ANONYMOUS

When Moses an' his soldiers
f'om Egypt's lan' did flee
His enemies were in behin' him
An' in front of him de sea.
God raised de waters like a wall,
An' opened up de way,
an' de God dat lived in Moses' time
   is just de same today.

Response:
Is just de same today
Jus de same today.
An de God dat lived in Moses' time
   is just de same today.

Daniel faithful to his God,
would not bow down to men,
an' by God's enemy he was hurled
into de lion's den.
God locked de lion's jaw we read,
An' robbed him of his prey,
An de God dat lived in Daniel's time
   is just de same today.

Response:
Is just de same today,
jus' de same today
An de God dat lived in Daniel's time
   is jus' de same today.

IN *The Book of American Negro Spirituals*, from which this selection has been taken, the music for these lyrics was arranged by J. Rosamund Johnson. In the introduction to the collection, James Weldon Johnson emphasizes the originality and spiritual depth of the songs.

The story of Moses is told in Exodus, as well as in Leviticus and Numbers. The story of the parting of the waters so that the Israelites could cross the sea is in Exodus 14:21–30.

The story of Daniel is told in the Book of Daniel.

Night

PAUL LAURENCE DUNBAR

Silence, and whirling worlds afar
   Through all encircling skies.
What floods come o'er the spirit's bar,
   What wondrous thoughts arise.

The earth, a mantle falls away,
   And, winged, we leave the sod;
Where shines in its eternal sway
   The majesty of God.

RALPH HODGSON

He came and took me by the hand
   Up to a red rose tree,
He kept His meaning to Himself
   But gave a rose to me.

I did not pray Him to lay bare
   The mystery to me,
Enough the rose was Heaven to smell,
   and His own face to see.

Yet Do I Marvel

COUNTEE CULLEN

I doubt not God is good, well-meaning, kind,
And did He stoop to quibble could tell why
The little buried mole continues blind,
Why flesh that mirrors Him must some day die,
Make plain the reason tortured Tantalus
Is baited by the fickle fruit, declare
If merely brute caprice dooms Sisyphus
To struggle up a never-ending stair.
Inscrutable His ways are, and immune
To catechism by a mind too strewn
With petty cares to slightly understand
What awful brain compels His awful hand.
Yet do I marvel at this curious thing:
To make a poet black, and bid him sing.

LINE 5: Tantalus, a character in Greek mythology, is condemned to stand in water that recedes when he bends to drink and to look at a fruit tree that withdraws when he reaches for something to eat. His name is the source of the word *tantalize*.

Line 7: Sisyphus, a character in Greek mythology, is condemned to spend eternity rolling a stone up to the top of a hill, only to watch it escape his grasp and roll back to the bottom.

The Garments of God

JESSICA POWERS

God sits on a chair of darkness in my soul.
He is God alone, supreme in his majesty.
I sit at His feet, a child in the dark beside Him;
my joy is aware of His glance and my sorrow is tempted
to nest on the thought that His face is turned from me.
He is clothed in the robes of His mercy, voluminous
    garments—
not velvet or silk and affable to the touch,
but fabric strong for a frantic hand to clutch,
and I hold to it fast with the fingers of my will.
Here is my cry of faith, my deep avowal
to the Divinity that I am dust.
Here is the loud profession of my trust.
I need not go abroad
to the hills of speech or the hinterlands of music
for a crier to walk in my soul where all is still.
I have this potent prayer through good or ill:
here in the dark I clutch the garments of God.

JESSICA POWERS was a Carmelite nun when she described in a series
of poems what St. John of the Cross, the Carmelite mystic of the seven-
teenth century, called "the dark night of faith." The hiddenness of God
is not the absence of God.

Via Negativa

R. S. THOMAS

Why no! I never thought other than
That God is that great absence
In our lives, the empty silence
Within, the place where we go
Seeking, not in hope to
Arrive or find. He keeps the interstices
In our knowledge, the darkness
Between stars. His are the echoes
We follow, the footprints he has just
Left. We put our hands in
His side hoping to find
It warm. We look at people
And places as though he had looked
At them, too; but miss the reflection.

LINES 10–11: The image of putting our hands in God's side is drawn
from John 20:27, which describes Jesus' invitation to Thomas to
"reach out your hand and put it in my side" to verify that the Jesus
who was crucified has returned. The image of a hole in the side—es-
pecially the side of God—occurs frequently in the poetry of R. S.
Thomas. See "Cain" and "Soliloquy" in *H'm*, from which this selec-
tion is also taken.

Watchmaker God

ROBERT LOWELL

Say life is the one-way trip, the one-way flight,
say this without hysterical undertones—
then you could say you stood in the cold light of science,
seeing as you are seen, espoused to fact.
Strange, life is both the fire and fuel; and we
the animals and objects, must be here
without striking a spark of evidence
that anything that ever stopped living
ever falls back to living when life stops.
There's a pale romance to the watchmaker God
of Descartes and Paley; He drafted and installed
us in the Apparatus. He loved to tinker;
but having perfected what He had to do,
stood off shrouded in his loneliness.

LINE 10: William Paley was an eighteenth-century Anglican priest and Utilitarian philosopher who argued for the existence of God on the premise that both a watch and the world required a maker. The "watchmaker God" is the God of Deism.

JOHN FREDERICK NIMS

Nothing first-hand. I'm not your Saul. No burst
Of the Unendurable Dazzlement. Never durst
Claim more than a thrilling hunch: swirled autumn air,
Moon's stealth, or ado in the leaves—

shhh!

Someone there?

THE POET alludes to the conversion of Saul, later St. Paul, which is described dramatically in the Acts of the Apostles (9:3–4): "Suddenly a light from heaven flashed around him. He fell to the ground and heard a voice saying to him, 'Saul, Saul, why do you persecute me?'"

The Preacher: Ruminates behind the Sermon

GWENDOLYN BROOKS

I think it must be lonely to be God.
Nobody loves a master. No. Despite
The bright hosannas, bright dear-Lords, and bright
Determined reverence of Sunday eyes.

Picture Jehovah striding through the hall
Of His importance, creatures running out
From servant-corners to acclaim, to shout
Appreciation of His merit's glare.

But who walks with Him?—dares to take His arm,
To clap Him on the shoulder, tweak His ear,
Buy Him a Coca-Cola or a beer,
Pooh-pooh His politics, call Him a fool?

Perhaps—who knows?—He tires of looking down.
Those eyes are never lifted. Never straight.
Perhaps sometimes He tires of being great
In solitude. Without a hand to hold.

RICHARD WILBUR

Shall I love God for causing me to be?
I was mere utterance; shall these words love me?

Yet when I caused his work to jar and stammer,
And one free subject loosened all his grammar,

I love him that he did not in a rage
Once and forever rule me off the page,

But, thinking I might come to please him yet,
Crossed out *delete* and wrote his patient *stet*.

"Do you believe in a God
who can change the course of events
on earth?"
        "No, just
the ordinary one."
        A laugh,
but not so stupid: events
He does not, it seems, determine
for the most part. Whether He could
is not to the point; it is not
stupid to believe in
a God who mostly abjures.

The ordinary kind
of God is what one believes in
so implicitly that
it is only with blushes or
bravado one can declare,
"I believe"; caught as one is
in the ambush of personal history, so
harried, so distraught.

The ordinary kind
of undeceived believer
expects no prompt reward
from an ultimately faithful
but meanwhile preoccupied landlord.

DENISE LEVERTOV

As if God were an old man
always upstairs, sitting about
in sleeveless undershirt, asleep,
arms folded, stomach rumbling,
his breath from open mouth
strident, presaging death . . .

No, God's in the wilderness next door
—that huge tundra room, no walls and a sky roof—
busy at the loom. Among the berry bushes,
rain or shine, that loud clacking and whirring.
irregular but continuous;
God is absorbed in work, and hears
the spacious hum of bees, not the din,
and hears far-off
our screams. Perhaps
listens for prayers in that wild solitude.
And hurries on with the weaving:
till it's done, the great garment woven,
our voices, clear under the familiar
    blocked-out clamor of the task,
can't stop their
        terrible beseeching. God
imagines it sifting through, at last, to music
in the astounded quietness, the loom idle,
the weaver at rest.

ANNE SEXTON

My faith
is a great weight
hung on a small wire,
as doth the spider
hang her baby on a thin web,
as doth the vine,
twiggy and wooden,
hold up grapes
like eyeballs,
as many angels
dance on the head of a pin.

God does not need
too much wire to keep Him there,
just a thin vein,
with blood pushing back and forth in it,
and some love.
As it has been said:
Love and a cough
cannot be concealed.
Even a small cough.
Even a small love.
So if you have only a thin wire,
God does not mind.
He will enter your hands
as easily as ten cents used to
bring forth a Coke.

The Imperfect Paradise

LINDA PASTAN

If God had stopped work after the third day
With Eden full of vegetables and fruits,
If oak and lilac held exclusive sway
Over a kingdom made of stems and roots,
If landscape were the genius of creation
And neither man nor serpent played a role
And God must look to wind for lamentation
And not to picture postcards of the soul,
Would he have rested on his bank of cloud
With nothing in the universe to lose,
Or would he hunger for a human crowd?
Which would a wise and just creator choose:
The green hosannas of a budding leaf
Or the strict contract between love and grief?

But God Is Silent / Psalm 114

DANIEL BERRIGAN

Sotto voce
cynics pass the word —
Let's hear from your god
How many legions has he?

But god is silent
the creator of splendors
earth and heaven, a dazzle of stars
all creatures that fly, swim, walk
breathe and blossom
yes and simple unblinking stones
sun and moon, splendid beyond all telling
and the squat toad
the owl's myopic stare

This panoply, this outspread
banquet of sight and sound
and its silent
Maker
our momentous Friend
our androgynous Lover!

LINE 4: Cf. Matthew 26:53: "Do you think that I cannot appeal to my Father, and he will at once send me more than twelve legions of angels?" The line also alludes to Josef Stalin's reference to the power of the Pope: "How many divisions does he have?"

MARK JARMAN

God like a kiss, God like a welcoming,
God like a hand guiding another hand
And raising it or making it descend,
God like the pulse point and its silent drumming,
And the tongue going to it, God like the humming
Of pleasure if the skin felt it as sound,
God like the hidden wanting to be found
And like the joy of being and becoming.
And God the understood, the understanding,
And God the pressure trying to relieve
What is not pain but names itself with weeping,
And God the rush of time and God time standing.
And God the touch body and soul believe,
And God the secret neither one is keeping.

Naming the Living God

KATHLEEN NORRIS

"The Special Theory came to me,"
Einstein said,
"as shifting forms of light."
Riemann once remarked, "I did not
invent those pairs of differential equations, I found them
in the world,
where God had hidden them."

Natural numbers stand firm,
granite laced
with ice.
Negative numbers roam, lions
about to pounce.

All things change
when you measure them. You might as well
sing, the sound of your voice
joining the others, like waters overflowing
the name of the living God.

SARAH FLOWER ADAMS (1805–48) Born in Harlow, Essex, England, the daughter of an editor and publisher who once was sent to prison for writing a newspaper article criticizing a bishop, Sarah Flower Adams contributed thirteen hymns to a text published by a Unitarian society. She published prose and verse in a religious journal and wrote a religious dramatic poem entitled *Vivia Perpetua*, as well as a catechism for children called *The Flock at the Fountain*.

DANIEL BERRIGAN (b. 1921) A Jesuit priest, poet, writer, and activist, Berrigan was born in Two Harbors, Minnesota, and ordained in 1952. He studied in France and was an associate professor of theology at Le Moyne College in Syracuse, New York. His collection *Time Without Number* won the Lamont Poetry Award. For his protest efforts against the Vietnam War, he was arrested and eventually sentenced to eighteen months in prison for destroying draft registration files in Catonsville, Maryland. After his release in 1972, he was arrested several times for demonstrating against the production of weapons of war. He has written more than fifty books, including *The Trial of the Catonsville 9*, published in 1970.

JOHN BERRYMAN (1914–72) John Allyn Smith was born in McAlester, Oklahoma. After his father's suicide in 1926, his mother married John Angus McAlpin Berryman, who adopted her son. A brilliant scholar and teacher, Berryman published his first book of poems in 1942. After the publication of *Homage to Mistress Bradstreet* (1956), Berryman received a second Rockefeller scholarship and the Harriet Monroe poetry prize. He received the Pulitzer Prize in 1965 for *77 Dream Songs*. *His Toy, His Dream, His Rest* (1968) earned the National Book Award and the Bollingen Prize. *Love and Fame* was published shortly before the poet's suicide in 1972. *Delusions, etc.* was published posthumously.

WILLIAM BLAKE (1757–1827) More than a poet, Blake was an engraver, a painter, and a visionary who wrote, as he said, under the direction of "Messengers from Heaven." "The Divine Image" is taken from *Poetical Sketches*, a collection of his earliest poetry fairly conventional in style and content but anticipatory of later themes. In "The Marriage of Heaven and Hell," Blake asserts the necessity of uniting apparently contrary forces: reason and energy, love and hate. Humankind must resist the exaltation of reason and the limitations of conventional morality.

GWENDOLYN BROOKS (b. 1917) Born in Topeka, Kansas, Gwendolyn Elizabeth Brooks was the first African-American poet to win the Pulitzer Prize. Her collections of poetry, *A Street in Bronzeville*, *The Bean Eaters*, *Selected Poems*, and *In the Mecca,* focus on the lives of urban blacks. *Bronzeville Boys and Girls* is a book for children. During 1985–86 she was a consultant in poetry at the Library of Congress. She has been poet laureate of Illinois and professor of English at Chicago State University.

EMILY BRONTË (1818–48) The daughter of an Anglican parson, Emily Brontë spent most of her short life in Haworth in Yorkshire, England. Her aunt, a staunch Methodist, was instrumental in the education of Emily and her sisters, but Emily resisted formal religion. She was attracted to the God she experienced within nature, referring to organized religion as "a brotherhood of misery." She is famous for her novel, *Wuthering Heights*, published in the year of her death.

ELIZABETH BARRETT BROWNING (1806–61) The eldest of eleven children, Elizabeth Moulton Barrett, injured as a young girl, remained a semi-invalid for most of her life. Shortly after moving with her father to London, she began publishing poetry. In 1844 she met Robert Browning, with whom she eloped two years later. Her fame rests almost exclusively on the forty-five poems included in *Sonnets from the Portuguese*. Although deeply pious and profoundly interested in humanitarian causes, she objected to ritual and any intermediary between God and the individual human.

THOMAS CAMPION (1567–1620) Campion studied at Cambridge as an undergraduate, then studied law at Gray's Inn and eventually went to Europe to study medicine. A poet, musician, and physician, he published a series of songbooks, the *Book of Ayres* in 1601 and three succeeding volumes that contain the lyrics and music for about 150 songs. His poetry should be studied with his music. In *Observations on the Art of English Poesie*, he urged classical prosody over and against the accentual and rhymed verse characteristic of English poetry.

SAMUEL TAYLOR COLERIDGE (1772–1834) The most important theorist of the Romantic movement, Coleridge, born in London and orphaned as a child, led a troubled life characterized by sickness and instability. His fame rests on three brilliant poems ("Kubla Khan," "The Rime of the Ancient Mariner," and "Christabel") and *Biographical Literaria*, a philosophical treatise on the nature of poetry,

WILLIAM COWPER (1731–1800) A descendant on his mother's side of John Donne, Cowper was the son of a parson in Hertfortshire, England. Suffering severe depression as a young man, he attempted suicide and was hospitalized. His religious conversion occurred during his stay at St. Alban's sanitorium. Later he lived with friends and began writing hymns with a Calvinist preacher. In spite of recurring illness, he translated Homer and wrote confessional poetry as well as a long nature poem, *The Task*.

STEPHEN CRANE (1871–1900) An American novelist, short-story writer, and poet, Crane was born in Newark, New Jersey, and moved to New York City as a young man. There he wrote his first important literary work, *Maggie, A Girl of the Streets*. His second novel, *The Red Badge of Courage*, made him internationally famous. His collections of poetry include *The Black Riders* (1895) and *War Is Kind* (1899). He spent the last two years of his life in Europe.

RICHARD CRASHAW (c. 1613–49) Although the son of a militant Puritan cleric, Crashaw refused to subscribe to the Puritan covenant and was dismissed from his fellowship at Peterhouse College, Cambridge. He then traveled to Europe and subsequently converted to Roman Catholicism, even receiving from the Pope an ecclesiastical post in England. Considered the chief poet of the English Counter-Reformation, he is sometimes associated with the English metaphysical poets, but his emphasis on sensuous imagery links him to European baroque art.

COUNTEE CULLEN (1903–46) Cullen was born in Louisville, Kentucky, as Countee Leroy Porter. He was raised by his grandmother until he was adopted unofficially by Frederick A. Cullen, a minister of the Salem African Methodist Episcopal Church in Harlem. In 1925, the same year he graduated from New York University, he published his first collection of poetry, *Color*. Serving as assistant editor of *Opportunity: Journal of Negro Life*, he was active in the Harlem Renaissance, writing poetry and editing *Caroling Dusk*, an anthology of African - American poetry. A Guggenheim fellowship enabled him to live and write in France, and upon his return he taught in the New York City public schools. His later writings include three more volumes of poetry (*The Black Christ and Other Poems*, *The Medea and Some Poems*, *On These I Stand*); two children's books; a novel; and, in collaboration with Arna Bontemps, a musical play (*St. Louis Woman*).

DONALD DAVIE (1922–95) Born in Yorkshire, England, and a teacher at Cambridge and the University of Essex, which he helped establish, Davies was a principal figure in The Movement, a group of British poets in the 1950s who were antiromantic and opposed to experimentalism. He was a lecturer at Trinity College in Dublin and served on the faculties of Stanford and Vanderbilt Universities in the United States. His published works include criticism, translations, seven volumes of poetry, and numerous contributions to journals.

JOHN DAY (1574–c. 1640) John Day was born in Norfolk, England. He attended Cambridge University until 1593, when he was expelled for stealing a book. A few years later he began writing plays for a theater company owned by Philip Henslowe, working with a group of other hired playwrights that included Thomas Dekker. His most reputable play was *The Parliament of Bees*, a masque composed of pastoral eclogues. His other plays include *The Blind Beggar of Bednal-Green*, *The Isle of Gulls*, and *Humour Out of Breath*.

EMILY DICKINSON (1830–86) Living in seclusion in Amherst, Massachusetts, Emily Dickinson wrote more than 1,700 poems, only seven of which were published during her lifetime. The first volume of her poetry was published four years after her death, and she continues to rank among the greatest of American poets. Usually written in four-line stanzas, her poems are untitled. They are intense, sometimes cryptic, and brilliantly revelatory of states of mind. Her family tradition was Congregationalist, but her denominational loyalties were less than fervent. "I know that He exists," she wrote of God, "somewhere in silence."

JOHN DONNE (c. 1572–1631) Having converted from Roman Catholicism to Anglicanism in 1593, Donne was ordained in the Anglican church in 1615. He was Dean of St. Paul's in London from 1621 until his death. His poetry is usually grouped into three periods: from 1592, when he graduated from Oxford, until his marriage in 1601 to Anne More; from his marriage to his ordination; from his ordination to his death. His earlier poetry is distinctly secular, brilliantly complex, and often erotic. Donne is the most distinguished of a group of seventeenth-century poets later known as the Metaphysical poets.

PAUL LAURENCE DUNBAR (1872–1906) The child of former slaves, Dunbar was born in Dayton, Ohio, and published his first volume of poetry in 1893 at his own expense. Later his work attracted the attention of William Dean Howells, who wrote an introduction to *Lyrics of Lowly Life*. When his poetry about plantation life, often written in dialect, began to be popular, he was invited to give readings throughout the United States and England. Before his early death he published four novels and four collections of short stories.

RALPH WALDO EMERSON (1803–82) Emerson was born in Boston and educated at Harvard College and the Harvard Divinity School. His father had been a Unitarian minister, and Emerson attempted to follow in the same vocation, only to realize that his religious beliefs did not correspond to traditional doctrine. Access to God was through one's personal experience and interior revelation rather than through an established church or ritual. Emerson's influence on American literature and culture was extensive, particularly through the ideas articulated in his essay "Self-Reliance."

LOUISE GLÜCK (b. 1943) A Chancellor of the Academy of American Poets and winner of numerous literary awards, including the Pulitzer Prize for *The Wild Iris*, Louise Glück was born in New York City and grew up on Long Island. In addition to writing eight collections of poetry and contributing to numerous anthologies and periodicals, Glück has served as visiting professor at several American universities and colleges. She presently teaches at Williams College in Massachusetts.

THOMAS HARDY (1840–1928) Born in Dorsetshire, England, Hardy first achieved fame as a novelist. *Far from the Madding Crowd*, *The Return of the Native*, *The Mayor of Casterbridge*, and *Tess of the d'Urbervilles* were all financially and critically successful, but Hardy's resistance to Victorian religious conservatism, especially in *Jude the Obscure* (1895), alienated many of his contemporaries. After the hostile reception of that novel, Hardy devoted his creative energies to poetry for the rest of his life. *Wessex Poems* (1898) and *Poems of the Past and Present* (1901) are his two most important collections. *The Dynasts*, a long closet drama, examines the Napoleonic Wars in terms of his own philosophic conviction that human consciousness and human sensitivity must gradually inform the Universal Will.

GEORGE HERBERT (1593–1633) An Anglican pastor, George Herbert was born in Wales and served his church at Bemerton, near Salisbury. *The Temple: Sacred Poems and Private Ejaculations*, published shortly after his death, includes 160 poems. With this widely popular collection, Herbert became one of the most influential and revered religious poets of English history.

ROBERT HERRICK (1591–1674) Born in London, Herrick studied at Cambridge and began a career in law. He was more interested, however, in writing poetry and was deeply influenced by Ben Jonson, his mentor and friend. Ordained in the Anglican Church in 1627, he spent much of his life as a country pastor in Devonshire. Most of his poetry is hedonistic in the tradition of the Cavalier poets, who defended royalty, nature, love, and literature and whose world view was opposed by their Puritan political and religious enemies. Among the most famous of Herrick's 1,130 poems is "Gather ye Rosebuds While Ye May," a reflection of the classical *carpe diem* theme popular in the seventeenth century.

RALPH HODGSON (1872–1962) English by birth, Hodgson came to live in the United States in 1940, when he retired to a farm in Canton, Ohio, and started a small press. His lyric poetry is unforgettable in its simplicity and tenderness. His first published anthology (1907) was *The Last Blackbird and Other Lines*. A collected edition of his work was published in 1917, entitled *Poems*. He was known more as a breeder and judge of bull terriers than as a poet, partly because he refused to offer information about himself for literary reference books.

GERARD MANLEY HOPKINS (1844–89) Hopkins was born to Anglican parents in London and attended Balliol College at Oxford, where he studied under Walter Pater and Benjamin Jowett. The Tractarian Movement of intellectuals who were attempting to find a theological and religious "middle ground" between Roman Catholicism and the Protestant evangelical movement had left its conservative imprint on Oxford. John Henry Newman left that movement in 1845, converting to Roman Catholicism and subsequently influencing the young Hopkins, whom he received into the Church in 1866. Two years later Hopkins entered the Society of Jesus (Jesuits). He spent most of his clerical life as a teacher of classics at Stonyhurst College and at University College in Dublin. He died of typhoid fever. His poems remained unpublished until 1918, when his close friend Robert Bridges, then poet laureate, edited *The Poems of Gerard Manley Hopkins*.

MARK JARMAN (b. 1952) Born in Mount Sterling, Kentucky, Mark Jarman studied at the University of California–Santa Cruz and the University of Iowa. He is a professor of English at Vanderbilt University and the cofounder of the poetry journal *The Reaper* and of Story Line Press. He is the author of eight collections of poetry. *Questions for Ecclesiastes* won the Lenore Marshall Poetry Prize in 1998 and was a finalist for the National Book Critics Circle Award. Jarman's poetry and essays have been published widely.

BEN JONSON (1572–1637) Jonson, born in Westminster, England, achieved his first success as a playwright (*Every Man in His Humour*). After Shakespeare, he is considered the major dramatist during the reigns of Elizabeth I and James I. He wrote essays and criticism and more than thirty masques. He was the first (unofficial) poet laureate of England.

JACK KEROUAC (1922–69) Jean-Louis Kerouac was born in Lowell, Massachusetts, to French-Canadian parents. He attended Columbia University on a football scholarship but never graduated. Instead he signed up briefly with the merchant marine and began to write and eventually to travel haphazardly about the United States, associating all the time with friends who became known later as leading figures of the Beat generation. His travel narrative, *On the Road*, made him famous, attracting attention to a subculture of writers, folk singers, and marginalized types, some of whom, like William S. Burroughs, Allen Ginsberg, and Gary Snyder, became celebrated writers and poets. Before his death in St. Petersburg, Florida, Kerouac published seventeen books, including *The Dharma Bums* (1958), *The Subterraneans* (1958), *Doctor Sax* (1959), *Lonesome Traveler* (1960), and *Desolation Angels* (1965). *Visions of Cody* was published after his death.

RUDYARD KIPLING (1865–1936) In 1871 Kipling's parents brought him to England from Bombay, where he had been born. When he was seventeen, he returned to India and secured work in Lahore. He returned to England in 1889 and married, then lived in Vermont for several years with his American wife. His rhythmic ballads and ringing imperialism made his poetry immensely popular. He was the first Englishman to receive the Nobel Prize for literature. His novels include *Captains Courageous*, *The Jungle Book*, and *Kim*.

WALTER SAVAGE LANDOR (1775–1864) Expelled from Trinity College in Oxford for shooting at the window of another student, Landor traveled extensively, living in Florence for much of his life. He published poetry for more than sixty-eight years, attempting long blank verse epics but achieving his best work in short lyrics. "God Scatters Beauty," included in this anthology, was written in his old age. He is famous primarily for his prose, especially *Imaginary Conversations*, a collection of 152 invented dialogues between famous characters in history and myth.

D. H. LAWRENCE (1885–1930) The son of a teacher and an illiterate coal miner, and educated in Nottingham, England, David Herbert Richards Lawrence achieved his fame as a novelist. But he also wrote short stories, essays, travel accounts, thousands of letters, and poetry. He eloped to Italy in 1912 with Frieda Weekley (née von Richthoven), and the couple traveled extensively, returning to England only occasionally. Lawrence died in Vence, France.

DENISE LEVERTOV (1923–97) Levertov was born in County Essex, England. Her father was a converted Russian Jew who was ordained to the Anglican priesthood the year before she was born. Her Welsh mother gave her a wide education in literature and languages at home. In 1948 she moved to the United States, becoming a naturalized citizen eight years later. She wrote more than twenty volumes of poetry and published poetry translations, collections of essays, and edited anthologies. Influenced by William Carlos Williams and the Black Mountain School of poetry, she experimented with form, always adjusting it to content and keeping content close to the events of everyday life. She was especially well known for her antiwar lectures and poetry during the Vietnam era. Although she described herself as an agnostic for most of her life, her admiration for Dorothy Day, Thomas

Merton, and Oscar Romero led her to Roman Catholicism and eventual conversion.

ROBERT LOWELL (1917–77) Born in Boston into a family already distinguished in American arts and letters, Lowell left Harvard, rejecting the Puritan/Calvinist tradition of his heritage and the Episcopalian religion of his parents, to study with Allen Tate. He converted to Roman Catholicism in 1940. After graduating from Kenyon College, he began publishing poetry, receiving the Pulitzer Prize in 1947 for *Lord Weary's Castle*. His later collections include *Life Studies* and *For the Union Dead* An editor, translator, critic, and dramatist, Lowell consistently reflected in his writing his own life experiences and his cultural and religious conflicts. His conversion to Catholicism had lasted only briefly.

HENRY F. LYTE (1793–1847) A curate in Devonshire, England, Lyte was born in Scotland and educated in Ireland. He had won college prizes for poetry and did not turn to writing hymns until later in his life. "Abide with Me" and "Praise My Soul, the King of Heaven" quickly became universal favorites and are still included in hymnals of every denomination.

JOHN MILTON (1608–74) Born in London, Milton attended Christ's College, Cambridge. Politics and religion dominated his life and writing. An ardent supporter of the Puritan Commonwealth, Milton held essentially Calvinist religious beliefs, although he rejected the doctrine of predestination. *Paradise Regained* was written as a short sequel to *Paradise Lost* and was published in 1671 together with *Samson Agonistes*.

SIR THOMAS MORE (1478–1535) The first layman to be appointed Lord High Chancellor of England, Thomas More resigned his office rather than take the Oath of Supremacy, which declared Henry VIII the ruler of the Church in England. For this refusal, More was sent to the Tower and later beheaded. He was beatified in 1886 and canonized in 1935. His major literary work is *Utopia*, the description of an ideal state governed by rational, humanistic principles.

PAUL MURRAY (b. 1947) A Dominican priest, Paul Murray was born in Newcastle, County, Down, Northern Ireland and educated at St. Malachy's College, Belfast. He entered the Dominican Order in 1966. His collections of poetry include *Ritual Poems*, *Rites and Meditations*, and *The Absent Fountain*. He is the author of two other books, *The*

Mysticism Debate and *T. S. Eliot and Mysticism*. He is a lecturer in mystical theology at the Dominican Studium in Tallaght, Ireland, and the Angelicum University in Rome.

MARILYN NELSON (b. 1946) Born in Cleveland and educated at the University of California–Davis, Marilyn Nelson has published verse for children, translations from Danish and German, and four volumes of poetry: *For the Body*, *Mama's Promises*, *The Homeplace*, and *Magnificat*. She was a National Book Award finalist in 1991.

JOHN HENRY NEWMAN (1801–90) As a young Anglican cleric, Newman, born in London and educated at Oxford, initially resisted Roman Catholicism, but he later converted and was received into the Church in 1845. He was ordained a priest and continued to preach and write. His sermons have become spiritual classics. His most famous prose works are *Apologia pro vita sua* (Explanation of his life) and *The Idea of a University*. His most significant religious work is *An Essay in Aid of a Grammar of Assent*, which examines the nature of religious belief. He was made a Cardinal of the Catholic Church before his death and is regarded as "Venerable," a designation that anticipates possible beatification.

JOHN FREDERICK NIMS (1913–99) Author of eight books of poetry and several translations, John Frederick Nims was born in Muskegon, Michigan, and studied at the University of Notre Dame and the University of Chicago. He was the editor of *Poetry* magazine from 1978 to 1984. His translations include *Sappho to Valery: Poems in Translation*, *Poems of St. John of the Cross*, and *The Complete Poems of Michelangelo*. He edited the *Harper Anthology of Poetry* and *Western Wind: An Introduction to Poetry*. Among his awards are the O. B. Hardison Poetry Prize from the Folger Library in 1993.

KATHLEEN NORRIS (b. 1947) An award-winning poet and essayist, and manager of a family ranch corporation, Norris was born in Washington, D.C., lived in New York, Vermont, and Honolulu, and eventually moved to her family home in South Dakota, a transition that inspired her book of essays, *Dakota: A Spiritual Geography*. She is also the author of *The Cloister Walk*, *Amazing Grace: A Vocabulary of Faith*, and *The Quotidian Mysteries*. She has published five books of poetry. In 1986 she became a Benedictine oblate, or lay associate, of the Order of St. Benedict.

ALICIA OSTRIKER (b. 1937) A professor of English at Rutgers University, Alicia Ostriker was born in Brooklyn and received her doctorate from the University of Wisconsin. She is the author of eight volumes of poetry, including *Green Age* and *The Crack in Everything*. Much of her work emphasizes the role of the Jewish woman and Jewish social and religious concerns. Her prose works include *The Nakedness of the Fathers: Biblical Visions and Revisions*; *Feminist Revisions and the Bible*; and *Stealing the Language: The Emergence of Women Poets in America*.

LINDA PASTAN (b. 1932) Linda Olenick Pastan was born in New York City and educated at Radcliffe, Simmons College, and Brandeis University. She won the Dylan Thomas Poetry Award from *Mademoiselle* in her senior year in college (Sylvia Plath was the runner-up). She married and began to raise a family before returning to poetry. In 1983 *PM/AM: New and Selected Poems* was nominated for the American Book Award. Pastan has published four other volumes of poetry, and lectures at the Breadloaf Writers Conference.

ALEXANDER POPE (1688–1744) Born in London, Pope was forced to live most of his life outside the city because of multiple restrictions against Roman Catholics. He became the most acclaimed poet of his age, despite poor health and a painful tubercular condition that left him with a severe spinal curvature. Pope wrote pastorals, a brilliant mock-epic ("The Rape of the Lock"), a poem on critics and critical taste ("An Essay on Criticism"), satires, ethical epistles, essays, and translations of Homer. He was a master of the heroic couplet, composing almost exclusively in that form. Philosophically, Pope was a Deist, arguing consistently for a divine order in the universe and the importance of reason.

JESSICA POWERS (1905–88) Born in the Cat Tail Valley of western Wisconsin, Jessica Powers lived and wrote in New York in the 1930s. In 1941 she entered a Carmelite monastery near Milwaukee and was known as Sister Miriam of the Holy Spirit. Her poems were collected and published under the title *The Place of Splendor*.

CHRISTINA GEORGINA ROSSETTI (1830–94) A devout Anglican and sister of Dante, the pre-Raphaelite painter, the London-born Christina was often a model for artists of the Pre-Raphaelite Brotherhood. Her collection *Goblin Market and Other Poems* was extremely popular, as was her devotional poetry, which often expressed her desire to renounce the world and her fear that she was not sufficiently detached from it. She dedicated her life to works of charity and to religious devotions.

ANNE SEXTON (1928–74) Anne Gray Harvey was born in Newton, Massachusetts. She attended Garland Junior College for a year, then married Alfred M. Sexton II. She suffered emotional disturbances and attempted suicide several times before finally taking her life by carbon monoxide poisoning in 1974. Her subject matter—often about women's lives and bodies—was sometimes criticized, but her extraordinary skill soon brought her international recognition. She won the Pulitzer Prize for poetry in 1966 for *Live or Die*. In addition to twelve books of poetry, her published works include essays, letters, and one play.

EDMUND SPENSER (1552–99) Born in London, Spenser graduated from Pembroke College, Cambridge, but lived in Ireland most of his life, working in various government posts. His most famous poetic achievement is *The Faerie Queene*, a massive project that was originally designed to present the culture and civilization of an entire age in a series of twenty-four books. He completed six. Spenser's poetic genius and his capacity to blend the archaic and the innovative launched English poetry onto the world scene, making him one of the most influential poets in English history.

TRINIDAD TARROSA SUBIDO (b. 1912) The editor, with Carolyn Fosdick, of a four-volume series, *Literature for Philippine High Schools*, Shanghai-born Trinidad Subido has published a selection of her own poems and those of her husband, Abelardo Subido, in *Two Voices: Selected Poems*. She is also the author of *The Feminist Movement in the Philippines, 1905–1955*.

JOSUAH SYLVESTER [Joshua; Joshuah] (1563–1618) A native of Kent, England, Sylvester was a poet and translator best known for his translation from the French of a biblical epic, *The Divine Weekes and Workes of Guillaume de Saluste, Sieur du Bartas*. He described his occupation as "merchant-adventurer."

EDWARD TAYLOR (1645–1729) Born into a nonconformist family near Coventry, England, Taylor emigrated to New England and was quickly enrolled in Harvard College. In 1671 he went to Westfield, Massachusetts, to serve as minister and physician. His 400-page collection of poetry, composed in the metaphysical tradition, was donated to Yale University by his descendants, but it was not discovered until 1937 or published until 1939. Two hundred of his poems, collected under the title *Preparatory Meditations*, were written as prayers before receiving communion or the Lord's Supper. Others were included under the title *God's Determinations Touching His Elect*. *The Poems of Edward Taylor* (1963), edited by Donald E. Stanford, is a comprehensive edition.

ALFRED TENNYSON (1809–92) Known commonly as Alfred, Lord Tennyson after he was given the title of "Baron of Aldworth and Farringford," the writer of "The Charge of the Light Brigade" was Victorian England's most revered poet. His most famous works include *In Memoriam*, "Locksley Hall," *Idylls of the King*, and "Crossing the Bar." As poet laureate, he made himself the spokesman for an age, defending Victorian orthodoxy and the ethos of the English middle class. He is buried in the Poet's Corner of Westminster Abbey.

R. S. THOMAS (b. 1913) One of the leading religious poets of the twentieth century, Ronald Stuart Thomas was born in Cardiff, Wales, and was ordained to the Anglican priesthood in 1936. Serving as pastor to several Welsh parishes, he studied and learned to speak Welsh fluently. He has published eighteen volumes of poetry since 1946 and received the Queen's Gold Medal for Poetry in 1964. His poetry flows from the daily life, landscape, and countryside of Wales and is characterized by his resistance to what he once described as a "comfortable, conventional, simplistic view of God."

FRANCIS THOMPSON (1859–1907) Thompson was born in Preston, Lancashire, England, and was educated as a Roman Catholic. After abandoning the study of medicine, he went to London but was reduced to selling matches and newspapers to make a living. Wilfred Meynell published two of his poems in *Merry England*. Alice and Wilfred Meynell eventually cared for the impoverished Thompson, who had become addicted to opium during an illness, and in 1893 Meynell published a volume of Thompson's poems. Later the poet lived in Wales, publishing two more volumes of poetry, *Sister Songs* and *New Poems*. *The Works of Francis Thompson* was published in 1893.

JAMES THOMSON (1700–48) Famous as a nature poet, Thomson was born in Ednam, Scotland, and educated at Edinburgh. He moved to London in 1725. His long series of poems entitled *The Seasons*, published in 1744, was one of the most popular texts of the eighteenth century. His poetic diction is expansive and elegant, exemplifying what Wordsworth would later criticize and resist in his own poetry. He is credited with the composition of "Rule, Brittania!" first sung in the second act of *Alfred: A Masque*, which he wrote in collaboration.

CHARLES ALBERT TINDLEY (1859–1933) Charles Tindley, the son of slaves, was born in Berlin, Maryland. He taught himself to read and write, attended night school while working as a janitor, and was ordained to the Methodist ministry. He eventually became the pastor of the church in Philadelphia where he had been the janitor, and which was eventually named after him. He was an extraordinarily successful preacher and hymn writer, composing more than forty-five hymns, the most famous of which was "I'll Overcome Someday," known now as "We Shall Overcome," the anthem of the civil rights movement. Other hymns include "We'll Understand It Better By and By" and "Take Your Burdens to the Lord."

THOMAS TRAHERNE (1637–74) Educated at Oxford, Traherne was ordained in 1660 and served as rector of Credenhill in Herefordshire and as chaplain to Sir Orlando Bridgeman in London. A devotional Anglican poet, he published only two minor prose works in his lifetime. Most of his poetry, including the collections *Poetical Works* and *Poems of Felicity*, was not discovered and published until the early twentieth century. His most important prose work is *Centuries of Meditations*.

HENRY VAUGHAN (1622–95) Born in Wales and educated at Oxford, Henry Vaughan became a physician. While still a young man he experienced a profound religious conversion, occasioned possibly by illness but also, according to Vaughan, a result of the influence of George Herbert's life and writing. He is classified among the Cambridge Platonists because of his emphasis on neoplatonic mysticism, the role of nature, and the privileged spirituality of childhood. His anthology *Silex Scintillans* (Sparks from the flint) includes all of his major poetry.

JONES VERY (1813–80) A Unitarian minister who studied at Harvard and spent most of his life in Salem, Massachusetts, Very believed that his poetry and all of his words had been inspired by the Holy Spirit. He preached throughout New England and attempted to become Emerson's spiritual director, believing that Emerson needed to see spiritual truth more clearly. Very was a strict interpreter of the Gospel, an absolutist in his sense of the divine call to obedience and submission. His quietism and the sobriety and purity of his diction gives his work spiritual depth, but his spirituality cannot be described as mystical or visionary. He wrote more than 700 poems, most of them in Shakespearean sonnet form.

ISAAC WATTS (1674–1748) Born in Southhampton, England, Watts was one of the greatest devotional poets of the eighteenth century. He wrote 761 hymns and psalms, including "Joy to the World"; 29 treatises on theology; numerous sermons; books on ethics, psychology, and education; and many poems and songs for children. His first collection of poetry, *Horae Lyricae*, was published in 1706 and was revised and extended the following year in the collection *Hymns and Spiritual Songs*. He was educated at the Stoke Newington Dissenting Academy, a school for those who objected to the remnants of Roman Catholicism in the Church of England. He eventually became pastor of the Independent Congregation (Congregationalist) in Mark Lane, London. When his health failed in 1712, he was invited to live with Sir Thomas Abney, a wealthy Dissenter, and he devoted the rest of his life to writing.

PHILLIS WHEATLEY (1753–84) Born in Senegal, West Africa, Phillis Wheatley was sold into slavery to the Boston family of John Wheatley, who taught her to read and write. She began writing poetry when she was fourteen years old, and in 1773 her *Poems on Various Subjects, Religious and Moral* was published in England. She was the first African-American poet in the United States. Her work attracted widespread attention in her own day, and in 1830 was cited by abolitionists as proof of the humanity and intelligence of blacks. When the Wheatley family dissolved, she married a freed black man, but died in poverty.

RICHARD WILBUR (b. 1921) The second poet laureate of the United States, Wilbur was born in New York City and educated at Amherst College and Harvard University. In 1957 he won the Pulitzer Prize for poetry and the National Book Award for poetry in 1957 for *Things of This World*. He won another Pulitzer Prize in 1989 for *New and Collected Poems*. He has published many translations, especially of French plays, and has written two books for children. He is the editor of *The Complete Poems of Poe* and *Poems of Shakespeare*. Considered one of the most distinguished poets of the United States, he has received numerous awards.